1001

PERENNIALS

1001
PERENNIALS

CLAIRE AUSTIN

B T Batsford Ltd • London

This book is for Ellen and Robert, my children.

First published in 2000
First published in paperback in 2003

ISBN 0 7134 8824 7

A CIP catalogue record for this book is available from the British Library.

Printed in Spain by Just Colour Graphics, S.L.

for the publishers

B T Batsford
64 Brewery Road
London N7 9NT
England
www.batsford.com

A member of **Chrysalis** Books plc

Distributed in the United States and Canada
by Sterling Publishing Co.,
387 Park Avenue South, New York, NY 10016, USA

MY PASSION FOR PERENNIALS began in my early teens at a time when, as a family, we lived on the Wrekin, one of Shropshire's most distinctive hills. Each school day, my friend Tanya and I would ride down the hill, on bikes, to catch the school bus. It was a route that took us through country lanes edged by wide verges containing a galaxy of wild flowers. Many of these were perennial and curiosity led me to look for their common names. As an interest, it proved invaluable for the years to come. From school, I moved to Bristol to study book illustration. Here, my tutors felt that I had a talent for botanical illustration, but this I stubbornly refused to embrace. It was simply too close to the interests of my parents: my father is a rose breeder and my mother a stone carver. However, a few years after leaving college, I found myself compiling and writing a catalogue of herbaceous perennials for the family business. After 12 editions, these, together with my interest in photography, have evolved into this book about perennial plants.

I can't imagine a garden without perennials. An enormous group of plants, it contains varieties for all seasons and aspects of the garden. No flower or 'cottage' garden could exist without them. Although I describe a thousand and one plants, this is only a very small proportion of the varieties that are available to gardeners today. Choosing such a limited number was no easy task and it struck me, while selecting them, that a definitive collection would be almost impossible to compile. Each year I discover new varieties, many of them introduced by plantsmen and nurserymen from around the world. Therefore, there were two criteria used for this selection: all the plants should be readily available and also be 'good' garden plants.

What do I mean by a 'good' garden plant? These are varieties that, given the right conditions, are reliable performers. To discover which were most readily available, I referred to the *RHS Plant Finder*. This, together with frequent visits to garden centres, proved an excellent guide. Each variety included is listed alphabetically by its Latin name. Although these can be tongue twisters, I consider them to be essential, if only because common names are tremendously variable, not only from region to region, but around the globe.

Finally, I would like to point out that this is an unashamedly English book. Having spent over 15 years selling perennials in Shropshire and growing them in various gardens, my experience is localised to the West Midlands of England. The descriptions are, however, first-hand and I hope that the following information will assist and enthuse both the new and experienced gardener alike.

WHAT IS A PERENNIAL?

Speaking botanically, perennials are plants that live for more than two years and naturally include trees and shrubs. However, to gardeners and horticulturists, the term 'Perennial' refers to plants which are herbaceous in nature, and perennial. Perhaps this book should have been called '1001 Herbaceous Perennials', but what a mouthful! Herbaceous plants, unlike trees and shrubs, produce soft stems that die back each winter and re-emerge the following spring. There are exceptions, and I have included a few – you will find plants that are evergreen, biennial or short-lived, and one or two that are technically called 'subshrubs'. These are grown and treated just like perennials.

HOW TO CHOOSE PERENNIALS

Choosing from a long list, be it from a book or a catalogue, can be a bewildering task. Therefore, knowing where to begin not only makes life easier, it is also essential if expense and disappointment are to be avoided. The following suggestions are merely guidelines for selecting the right plant for the right place.

SOIL

The first step in choosing the right plant for the correct position is to know your soil type. Plants can then be chosen that should always succeed, providing they receive the required amount of light. One thing to remember is that no two gardens are alike, and even within a garden, the type of soil can vary.

WELL-DRAINED SOILS

The majority of the plants described in this book will grow in a good, well-drained soil. These are soils that drain well even after heavy rain, contain an ample amount of nutrients and a balanced pH. Nutrients are essential to all plants and a good soil will contain a balance of these. The pH of a soil refers to how acid or alkaline it is. More technically minded publications will explain how to identify your soil more precisely. Soil types include chalk soils, clay soils, organic-based soils (peat and humus-rich) and sandy soils. The following categories are a general guide only.

WET SOILS

These are soils that remain wet or moist, even during hot summers. They are usually found around, or near ponds and streams, and include boggy situations.

DRY SOILS

A dry soil is most definitely a disadvantage. They are often poor in nutrients and during hot spells become so hard that the plants can suffer. These can be found beneath trees and shrubs, along the edges of stone and brick walls and on banks. Chalky and very sandy soils also tend to be dry.

POOR SOILS

An easy way to recognise a poor soil is to look at the existing vegetation, which is often sparse and appears starved. Dry soils, therefore, need special attention. They can be enriched by digging in a large amount of organic matter, such as horse manure. However, this is labour-intensive work, and for those who have limited time, it may be simpler to choose varieties that will adapt to poor conditions.

PLANTS FOR WET AND BOGGY AREAS

Astilbe
Caltha
Carex
Darmera
Filipendula
Hosta
Iris ensata
Iris laevigata
Iris pseudocorus
Ligularia
Lobelia
Lysimachia
Lythrum
Osmunda
Primula
Rodgersia
Scrophularia
Trollius

DRY SOILS

Acanthus
Anemone
Artemisia
Baptisia
Chelone
Digitalis
Echinops
Epimedium
Euphorbia
Geranium macrorrhizum
Gypsophila
Iris
Lamium galeobdolon 'Florentinum'
Lychnis coronaria
Matthiola
Pilosella
Rhodiola
Sedum
Trachystemon

POOR SOILS

Acanthus
Achillea
Carlina
Centranthus
Cichorium
Echinops
Epilobium
Eriophyllum
Erysimum
Galega
Hesperis
Knautia
Lamium
Linaria
Lychnis coronaria
Oenothera
Origanum
Plantago
Salvia sclarea
Saxifraga
Senecio
Stachys cretica
Verbascum

LIGHT

Plants need sunlight to thrive and some need more than others. If a plant needing full sun is grown in shade, it will become distorted or even die. The majority of varieties described in this book are happy in a sunny situation or one that has partial shade during the day.

Full sun
A site with full sun is a position that receives sunshine throughout the whole day.

Partial shade
These are sites that get some sunlight for a good proportion of the day.

Dappled shade
These are situations where overhanging trees or shrubs provide a light covering of shade most of the time.

Shade
Full shade, like poor soil, has limited scope for gardeners. Despite this, there is a wide choice of plants that can be grown, many of which are spring-flowering varieties.

PLANTS FOR SHADY AREAS, GENERALLY WITH MOIST SOIL

Aquilegia
Aruncus
Astilbe
Bergenia
Brunnera
Cimicifuga
Convallaria
Dicentra
Epimedium
Euphorbia amygdaloides robbiae
Gentiana asclepiadea
Geranium himalayense 'Gravetye'
Geranium macrorrhizum hybrids
Geranium nodosum
Geranium phaeum hybrids
Geranium versicolor
Helleborus
Hosta
Iris foetidissima
Kirengeshoma
Lamium
Leucojum
Lunaria
Meconopsis
Melittis
Omphalodes
Podophyllum
Persicaria
Primula
Pulmonaria
Smilacina
Smyrnium
Symphytum
Tellima
Trachystemon
Trillium
Uvularia
Veratrum
Waldsteinia

HARDINESS

The vast majority of perennials described in this book will cope with temperatures as low as –15 C (5 F). However, the following are rather more tender and may suffer if the temperature drops below –5 C (23 F) for any length of time. To prevent damage, these can be protected in cold districts with a thick covering of mulch.

Agastache
Alstroemeria
Cosmos atrosanguinea
Crocosmia (some hybrids)
Dierama
Ferula communis
Francoa
Gunnera manicata
Libertia
Lobelia tupa
Nerine
Phormium
Romneya coulteri
Salvia uliginosa
Schizostylis
Verbena bonariensis

CONSIDERING PLANTS

Flowers and foliage

Having established the soil type and the availability of light, the final and most exciting consideration is to choose the plants. Plants are made up of both flowers and leaves, an obvious statement you might think, but it is a fact that many gardeners often forget. Flowers are the first and most immediate reason for choosing a variety, but leaves (more often than not) will emerge well before the flowers and last until the frosts arrive, often with colourful results. Therefore, when considering what to choose, think about leaves, as well as flowers.

Shape

The shape of a plant is essential when considering which varieties to grow together. Tall varieties will hide smaller ones if planted in front of them. Robust, spreading varieties can smother delicate, less vigorous plants if they are placed beside one another. Therefore, take a note of how vigorous a variety is, or is not.

Tall plants for the back of a border

To get the most out of a plant it needs to be seen and the following, believe me, will be. They can also be used to hide unsightly views.
Alcea rosea
Boltonia
Campanula (some types)
Cephalaria
Crambe
Cynara cardunculus
Delphinium
Digitalis purpurea hybrids
Foeniculum vulgare 'Purpureum'
Helianthus
Inula magnifica
Macleaya
Rudbeckia 'Herbstsonne'
Salvia uliginosa
Senecio
Thalictrum
Verbascum olympicum
Veronicastrum

Plants for the front of a border

Placing plants at or towards the front of the border is like putting on a nice coat. It is often the first thing you see, introducing the eye to what is to come next. Of course, any size of plant can be placed at the front, but the following are small enough to allow most others to be seen.

Alchemilla
Anthemis punctata cupaniana
Bergenia
Campanula glomerata hybrids
Centaurea montana hybrids
Dicentra formosa hybrids
Erigeron
Euphorbia dulcis 'Chameleon'
Geranium (some types)
Geum
Heuchera
Hosta (some types)
Knautia macedonica
Lamium maculatum hybrids
Nepeta x faassenii
Oenothera fruticosa 'Fyrverkeri', macrocarpa, speciosa 'Siskiyou'
Origanum
Persicaria affinis 'Superba'
Potentilla
Primula vulgaris types
Prunella
Pulmonaria
Salvia x superba hybrids
Saxifraga
Scabiosa
Sedum (some types)
Stachys byzantina hybrids
Tiarella
Viola
Waldsteinia

Plants for covering ground

In my experience, if a space is tightly filled with plants, the ground will be covered sufficiently to exclude weeds. However, if an area needs to be colonised quickly, the following are tough, spreading varieties. Being natural thugs, only a few of each will be required to do the job.

Aegopodium
Ajuga
Convallaria
Euphorbia amygdaloides robbiae
Fragaria
Galium
Geranium macrorrhizum hybrids
Lamium hybrids, except L. orvala
Pachysandra
Persicaria
Phuopsis
Prunella
Stachys byzantina hybrids
Symphytum hybrids, except S. rubrum
Trachystemon
Waldsteinia

Evergreen plants

Plants with leaves that remain throughout winter are very useful. The following varieties will keep much of their foliage in an excellent state. There are others, such as Hemerocallis or Stachys byzantina, that remain in a semi-evergreen state for most of the winter months.

Ajuga reptans hybrids
Anthemis punctata cupaniana
Bergenia
Carex
Epimedium (some types)
Eryngium agavifolium
Euphorbia (most types)
Helleborus
Heuchera 'Stormy Seas' & 'Green Ivory'
x Heucherella
Iris foetidissima
Kniphofia (some types)
Libertia
Liriope muscari
Morina
Ophiopogon planiscapus 'Nigrescens'
Pachysandra
Phlomis russelliana
Phormium
Sisyrinchium
Stipa gigantea
Stachys cretica
Tellima
Waldsteinia

Plant for containers

Technically, all herbaceous plants can be grown in containers, providing the pots are large enough. However, the following varieties produce highly decorative foliage and combine well with each other. When placing in containers, be sure to supply lots of water and good drainage. Also bear in mind that most plants need frequent feeding and dividing or replacing every two or three years.

Agapanthus
Ajuga
Bergenia
Clematis
Cosmos
Dianthus
Eryngium
Euphorbia
Fragaria
Francoa
Gaura
Heuchera
x Heucherella
Hosta
Lamium
Liriope
Matthiola
Nerine
Ophiopogon
Origanum
Penstemon
Scabiosa
Tanacetum parthenium 'Rowallane'
Viola riviniana

Fragrance

Fragrance should never be overlooked. Not all plants are scented, but with just one or two specimens a further dimension will be added to the garden. Remember, fragrance is found in both flowers and leaves.

PLANTS WITH FRAGRANT FLOWERS

Aster sedifolius
Cimicifuga
Clematis heracleifolia 'Côte d'Azur'
Clematis recta
Convallaria
Cosmos
Crambe cordifolia
Dianthus
Eupatorium
Filipendula
Galium
Hemerocallis (by variety)
Hesperis
Hosta plantaginea japonica
Iris (Bearded types by variety)
Lunaria
Matthiola
Oenothera stricta
Paeonia (by variety)
Perovskia
Phlox
Primula chionantha
Primula florindae
Primula veris
Smilacina
Tellima grandiflora 'Odorata'
Valariana

PLANTS WITH FRAGRANT LEAVES

Agastache
Anthemis
Calamintha
Dictamnus
Foeniculum
Galium
Geranium macrorrhizum
Nepeta
Monarda
Origanum
Phuopsis

CULTIVATION AND MAINTENANCE

PLANTING

First things first. The actual planting of perennials will, naturally, depend on the variety. Some, like Irises and Peonies, require more specialised treatment and I have given instructions for these within the relevant description. Otherwise, it is a simple process.
1. Firstly, make sure the plant's roots and the soil around them is moist. Dig a hole big enough to accommodate these up to where the stems begin to emerge. With varieties purchased in containers, simply make sure the original compost is covered.
2. Place the plant within the hole and refill it with soil. Firm this gently, but do not compact it too much. If it is compressed too tightly around the plant, water may be prevented from getting to the roots. Composts and fertiliser are not generally required, particularly if the soil is open and moist. Indeed, most perennials resent being pampered.
3. It is very important to make sure that the plants are kept moist for the next few days, especially during warm, dry weather.

DEAD-HEADING AND CUTTING BACK

The tasks of dead-heading and cutting back the foliage are done in late winter before the new growth is produced in spring. I almost never fuss with my perennials at other times of the year, except to remove, in early summer, any spent flowers. This will encourage further blooms. However, some varieties are abundant in their seed production and if the seed heads are left on the plant these will scatter their contents freely. This can be a great asset if natural drifts of plants such as Foxgloves are required. There are also varieties where dead-heading would be a positive shame as, if left, they make a dramatic contribution to a winter garden and provide food for hungry birds. In most cases the dead autumn foliage provides both the plant and over-wintering insects with protection during cold, harsh spells.

Plants with particularly attractive seed heads

Achillea
Echinops
Eryngium
Ferula
Foeniculum
Lunaria
Miscanthus
Onoponon
Papaver
Stipa
Veratrum

DIVIDING

Once planted, in a situation to suit them, most varieties can be left to their own devices. Many perennials, in particular the fast-growing ones, need to be divided about every three years. If this is neglected, they will begin to deteriorate or smother less robust varieties. The division of a plant is a simple process, and also a cheap way of increasing them.
1. To lift a mature clump, dig it out using a fork. Many books suggest that large clumps of plants should be split by placing two forks back to back. However, as I find this a difficult method, I use a very large carving knife to cut through the mound. Make sure each section has a good piece of root attached.
Once it is divided, replant it using the suggestions indicated in 'Planting'.

MOVING PLANTS AROUND THE GARDEN

Many gardeners do not realise how tough perennials are. Not only do they resent being pampered, they can be planted and replanted at almost any time of the year. I often move them around the garden even at the height of summer, but they must be well watered afterwards and kept moist in dry spells. This means that they will not suffer and should recover very quickly.

PESTS AND DISEASES

The vast majority of perennials are not troubled by pests and diseases. Where these are a problem, I have mentioned it within the plant description. In a country such as Britain, which is warm and wet, the pest that causes most problems, is the slug. These love the soft, succulent shoots of plants such as Hostas and Delphiniums. Aphids too are a problem, but these, like slugs, can naturally be controlled if birds, toads and frogs are encouraged into the garden. This avoids the use of chemicals, which I occasionally resort to when there are no alternatives, as in the case of fungal diseases such as Peony Wilt.

WILDLIFE IN THE GARDEN

A static environment, with no wind, rain or sun, is not what gardening is about. No garden can be without its bees, butterflies and birds, and the added delights of wildlife can be experienced by those who live in towns or the country alike. These creatures can be encouraged into a garden by planting only a few varieties. Unfortunately, for those who live in rural situations, some wildlife can be a nuisance – namely, rabbits and deer.

PLANTS TO ENCOURAGE BEES AND BUTTERFLIES

Aster
Calamintha
Centranthus
Chrysanthemum
Coreopsis
Echinacea
Echinops
Eryngium
Helenium
Knautia
Nepeta
Origanum
Salvia
Scabiosa
Sedum
Verbena bonariensis

PLANTS THAT RABBITS DON'T LIKE

Rabbits can massacre a garden, especially in early spring when the juicy new shoots emerge. However, they don't generally like plants with furry leaves or varieties with a bitter taste. Once a plant has matured, rabbits will move on to younger, sweeter-tasting varieties, but if they are hungry, nothing will stop them from sampling anything.
Aconitum
Aegopodium
Ajuga
Alchemilla
Anaphalis
Anemone
Aquilegia
Asphodeline
Astilbe
Brunnera
Clematis
Convallaria
Cortaderia
Crocosmia
Cynara
Digitalis
Epimedium
Eupatorium
Euphorbia
Helenium
Helianthus
Helleborus
Hosta
Houttuynia
Iris
Kirengeshoma

Kniphofia
Lamium
Leucojum
Lysimachia
Malva
Miscanthus
Nepeta
Omphalodes
Paeonia
Papaver
Persicaria
Phormium
Polygonatum
Rheum
Romneya
Saxifraga
Sisyrinchium
Stachys byzantina types
Tellima
Tradescantia
Trillium
Trollius

PLANTS THAT DEER DON'T LIKE

Unlike rabbits, my experience of deer is almost non-existent, but these, I believe, are good 'deer proof' plants.
Acanthus
Aconitum
Artemisia
Astilbe
Campanula
Carex
Centaurea
Cortaderia
Crocosmia
Dicentra
Digitalis
Epimedium
Euphorbia
Ferns
Festuca
Filipendula
Gaillardia
Geranium
Gunnera
Helianthus
Hosta
Iris
Kniphofia
Leucanthemum
Leucojum
Liriope
Lychnis coronaria
Melittis
Nepeta
Origanum

Paeonia
Papaver
Phormium
Polygonatum
Potentilla
Pulmonaria
Romneya
Rudbeckia
Salvia
Scabiosa
Sisyrinchium
Tellima
Thalictrum
Tiarella
Trillium
Veratrum

BUYING

Garden centres
These days the local garden centre is likely to be one that belongs to a large chain of retail shops. Therefore, through economic necessity, the choice of plants is often very limited and, although excellent in quality, most varieties are stocked only when in flower. These are aimed at impulse buyers, but they are an excellent way of filling empty spots in a border with varieties already in bloom. Of course, there are exceptions to this generalisation and privately owned garden centres do exist, stocking an excellent range of good quality plants throughout the year.

Small nurseries
Rarely as glamorous as Garden Centres, these are usually small, one-man establishments that provide a wonderful way of buying a wide range of plants throughout the year. Most can help customers with advice on the plants that they sell and many will offer a mail order service.

Mail order
For those gardeners who have limited time, live far from a good source of plants, or who are seeking particular varieties, mail order is an ideal way of buying plants. All mail order companies, as well as many small nurseries, produce a catalogue listing the varieties they sell. Mail order does have a few drawbacks due to the difficulty of sending plants in a box. These are despatched only during the dormant season (usually October to March) and are often sold in small sizes due to the cost of transport.

TERMS USED IN THIS BOOK

Flowering times

The time a plant will flower depends on where you live in the world and each region within a country. Even in Britain, 'early summer' can vary from mid May, in southeast England, to mid June, in northern Scotland. Therefore, the flowering times given are general.

Height

The heights given with each description are those I have seen a plant reach. These may vary according to the type of soil, the amount of moisture and the light available.

AGM

This is an abbreviation of 'Award of Garden Merit'. These are awarded by the Royal Horticultural Society after field trials to varieties considered to be 'good' garden plants. I would like to mention that I don't always agree with the findings!

Names

All the plants described within this book have had their names checked with those in the *RHS Plant Finder*. However, to make them less cumbersome, many of them have been edited. Officially all variants or cultivars of wild plants should contain one of these abbreviations; 'subsp.'(subspecies), 'f.'(form) or 'var.'(variety), but as most gardeners would almost never use these in general speech, they have been excluded.

ACANTHUS (Bear's Breeches)

These are the grandest of garden perennials and ideal subjects for large borders. They produce thick clumps of broad, glossy, deep green leaves and sturdy stems with dense, geometric spikes of flowers. The flowers are white and hidden beneath maroon hoods. As they originate from hot, dry areas of the Mediterranean, they should be grown in a well-drained soil, either poor or rich, in sun or partial shade. Midsummer.

mollis A plant with white flowers each covered with large, soft mauve hoods and leathery, deeply divided, shiny foliage. 120 cm (4 ft).

spinosus The flowers are similar to *A. mollis*, but its foliage is more finely divided and ends in small spikes, making it a less 'child friendly' plant. 120 cm (4 ft).

ACHILLEA (Yarrow)

These are a firm favourite of mine. Sturdy stems of small, papery flowers are held in clusters above thick clumps of decorative foliage that comes in two types: the softer more fluffy kind is ideal for the front of a border; and the upright, deeply divided forms are more suited to larger borders. Over the last decade or so, there has been a proliferation of new varieties, many of which have not survived. However, the ones that have, provide us with a range of good colours, where once only yellow, red or white existed. All varieties are easy to grow, especially in a poor soil, as long as it is well-drained, and in sun. Early to late summer.

'Apfelblute' Deep rosy pink flowers, significantly paling with age, are borne in broad heads above grey-green, fern-like foliage. 75 cm (2½ ft).

'Coronation Gold' Strong, upright stems are topped with wide heads of tiny, bright yellow flowers above a clump of broad, grey-green leaves. I leave the dead flowers, that fade to soft brown, *in situ* until the stems collapse, as they add shape to a winter border. 90 cm (3 ft).

'Feuerland' A short plant with large heads of scarlet flowers each with a small, yellow eye and soft feathery foliage. 45 cm (18 in).

'Forncett Fletton' A new variety from the nursery of John Metcalf. It produces large clumps with rich orange flowers and soft green foliage. 90 cm (3 ft).

Acanthus mollis

Acanthus spinosus

Achillea 'Apfelblute'

Achillea 'Coronation Gold'

Achillea 'Feuerland'

Achillea 'Forncett Fletton'

Achillea 'Lachsschönheit'

'Lachsschönheit' Large, flat heads of deep salmon-pink flowers fade to peach as other buds open. These create a two-tone effect against fluffy, mid-green foliage. 75 cm (2½ ft).

millefolium **'Cerise Queen'** A deep pink-red form of our native yarrow with soft green, divided leaves. It can be rather untidy. 45 cm (18 in).

'Moonshine' A low, round clump of soft, grey leaves bears its deep yellow flowers in flat heads. AGM. 45 cm (18 in).

ptarmica **'Compacta Nana'** Large, white flowers, with papery centres, borne in broad heads with mid-green leaves. It is suitable for siting at the front of a border. 45 cm (18 in).

ptarmica **'The Pearl'** Leafy, upright stems topped with clusters of double, white flowers that are shaped like neat, round buttons. This is a delightful 'cottage' plant that spreads freely in a border and blooms throughout summer. 60 cm (2 ft).

'Taygetea' Clusters of pale lemon flowers are tightly packed into small, flat heads above an upright clump of greyish foliage. 45 cm (18 in).

Achillea millefolium 'Cerise Queen'

Achillea ptarmica 'Compacta Nana'

Achillea ptarmica 'The Pearl'

Achillea 'Moonshine'

Achillea 'Taygetea'

Achillea 'Terracotta'

Aconitum x cammarum 'Bicolor'

'Terracotta' The flowers are terracotta at first, then pale with age to orange-yellow. They are borne, in broad heads, on stiff stems above grey-green foliage to form an open, airy clump. 75 cm (2½ft).

ACONITUM (Monkshood, Wolf's Bane)

I have never had any great affection for aconitums, probably due to their poisonous nature. Despite this, they are extremely handsome plants and ideal for adding height to a mixed border. The flowers are evenly distributed up straight stems and resemble large, drooping hoods, as their common name suggests. At the base a mound of deeply fingered, rich green leaves is produced. Aconitums can be left undivided for years and will grow in a well-drained soil, that does not dry out, in sun or partial shade. Midsummer to mid autumn.

'Bressingham Spire' Dense spikes of deep indigo blue flowers. AGM. 90 cm (3 ft).

x cammarum **'Bicolor'** White flowers with a violet-blue tinge to the edges of the hoods. AGM. 120 cm (4 ft).

carmichaelii **'Arendsii'** Compact spikes of large, deep violet-blue flowers with glossy, very deep green leaves. 120 cm (4 ft).

lycoctonum One of the tallest aconitums with long, cream flowers carried unevenly up slender stems that sway about in mid-air. 150 cm (5 ft).

Aconitum carmichaelii 'Arendsii'

Aconitum lycoctonum

Aconitum 'Bressingham Spire'

Aconitum 'Spark's Variety'

Aconitum napellus vulgare 'Carneum'

Agapanthus 'Blue Giant'

Agapanthus campanulatus albidus

Agapanthus Headbourne Hybrids

Aconitum 'Newry Blue'

Aegopodium podagaria 'Variegatum'

'Spark's Variety' The growth habit of most blue varieties is similar to delphiniums, straight and upright. However, this is more open and carries its large deep violet-blue flowers on widely branched stems. It is the earliest *aconitum* to flower. AGM. 150 cm (5 ft).

napellus vulgare **'Carneum'** Palest pink, almost white, flowers with pink veining and purple stems. 150 cm (5 ft).

'Newry Blue' Mid-blue flowers are borne on very branched stems with dark green foliage. 90 cm (3 ft).

AEGOPODIUM *podagaria* **'Variegatum'** (Variegated Ground Elder)

Soft green and white leaves form a low, weed, excluding carpet with umbels of small, white flowers carried on upright stems. This is a variegated form of the justifiably much-berated weed. However, I have seen it grown with great effect in Monet's garden in Giverny, France and at Wollerton Hall in Shropshire, where it was planted under shrubs to lighten up a shady area. Grow in sun or shade, where the soil does not dry out. Summer. 45 cm (18 in).

AGAPANTHUS (Blue African Lily)

These elegant plants are ideal for containers and warm borders. Starry, trumpet-like flowers are held in loose umbels on tall, smooth, upright stems above a clump of straplike leaves. There are many hybrids, but as they originate from South Africa, many are not hardy enough for temperate areas. The ones I have chosen will survive in warmer areas of Britain. Be sure to buy mature plants, as they need to be large enough to bloom. Grow in any well-drained soil, in sun. Late summer.

'Blue Giant' This forms a large, round ball with mid-blue flowers. Each petal is marked with a darker rib. 120 cm (4 ft).

campanulatus albidus Flat, umbels of purest white flowers. 60 cm (2 ft).

Headbourne Hybrids This is one of the hardiest varieties with soft blue flowers. The colour tends to be variable, as it is often produced from seed. 60 cm (2 ft).

'Lilliput' Brilliant deep blue, loosely formed flowers. 45 cm (18 in).

'White Superior' Large round flowers of pure white. 90 cm (3 ft).

AGASTACHE

A subtle, upright, bushy plant with very small, mint-shaped flowers that are highly attractive to bees and butterflies. Its leaves are soft green and exude a powerful minty scent if brushed against. Plant in any well-drained soil, in sun. Summer.

foeniculum Short, tight spikes of mauve flowers are borne on leafy stems. 90 cm (3 ft).

rugosa Light blue flowers poke out of lilac-blue bracts to form short spikes on erect stems. Its leaves are thick, shiny and light green. 90 cm (3 ft).

AJUGA (Bugle)

I have not included many plants that grow below one foot in height, but I consider these native European weeds to be some of the most useful. Bugles produce short pyramids of small flowers above long, oval, evergreen foliage. These quickly form a creeping, ground-covering carpet that I allow to mingle, at the front of a border, with other low growing plants, such as lamiums. However, they are rather rampant, so make sure they do not smother more delicate plants. Grow in any soil that does not become too dry, in sun or shade. Early to late spring.

reptans **'Atropurpurea'** Shiny, beetroot-red foliage with rich blue flowers. AGM. 15 cm (6 in).

reptans **'Catlin's Giant'** Very handsome large, shiny, rich purple leaves, green beneath, produce short stems of blue flowers. AGM. 15 cm (6 in).

reptans **'Multicolor'** Blue flowers and shiny red leaves mottled with green and cream. 15 cm (6 in).

Agapanthus 'Lilliput'

Agapanthus 'White Superior'

Agastache foeniculum

Agastache rugosa

Ajuga reptans 'Atropurpurea'

Ajuga reptans 'Multicolor'

Ajuga reptans 'Catlin's Giant'

Alcea rosea

Alcea rosea 'Chater's Double'

Alcea rosea 'Nigra'

ALCEA (Hollyhock)

Hollyhocks have been the symbol of the cottage garden since the middle of the 19th century. This is evident when you look at Victorian watercolour paintings of cottages. The walls are dressed with these tall, elegant plants, their strong stems bursting with large, open, trumpet-shaped flowers above a clump of round, mid-green leaves. Today they still evoke the same feeling of quaintness. However, treat them as short-lived perennials, or even biennials, and allow them to set seed. They are at their best in drier soils, in sun. Summer.

rosea Large, single, disclike flowers are produced in a range of colours, including white, lemon, pink and red. 240 cm (8 ft).

rosea **'Chater's Double'** Flat pompons, all ruffled in the centre, open at intervals up tall stems in every pastel and bright colour imaginable. 240 cm (8 ft).

rosea **'Nigra'** Large, single, dark red flowers. A rather unusual colour. 240 cm (8 ft).

ALCHEMILLA (Lady's Mantle)

These are essential plants for the flower garden with fluffy clouds of tiny, green-yellow flowers and mounds of round leaves, perfectly scalloped around the edges. They are wonderful for blending with other perennials or shrub roses and for softening the edges of paving and patios. Grow in any well-drained soil, in sun or partial shade. Early summer.

conjuncta A low, mounding plant with shiny, deep green leaves, silver beneath and around the edges. It produces clusters of tiny, lime-green flowers. 23 cm (9 in).

mollis In my opinion, this is one plant that cannot be left out of any garden. Its soft, round leaves form beautiful clumps, while the large, fluffy heads of green-yellow flowers are some of the most valuable material for cutting to put in vases. Beware, this is a prolific self-seeder, so cull where necessary. AGM. 45 cm (18 in).

Alchemilla conjuncta

Alchemilla mollis

Alstroemeria aurea

Alstroemeria ligtu

Amsonia orientalis

Amsonia tabernaemontana salicifolia

ALSTROEMERIA (Peruvian Lily)

Very much a florists' flower. The delicate trumpet-shaped blooms are borne in open sprays on long stems with just a few leaves. When happy, the fleshy roots will spread with vigour, especially in a good fertile soil. Don't divide them, as they like to be abandoned. Grow in a very well-drained soil, in sun. Summer.

aurea A vigorous variety with soft orange flowers. 90 cm (3 ft).

ligtu hybrids A cross between two not terribly hardy species with flowers in shades of soft pink or yellow. It needs a sheltered site to be successful. AGM. 90 cm (3 ft).

AMSONIA (Blue Star)

These unpretentious plants form upright clumps with slender stems of pointed leaves and clusters of little, starry, blue flowers. They are neat plants for the front of a border and will grow in any reasonably moist, yet well-drained, soil, in sun. Summer.

orientalis Stems of oval, pointed, mid-green leaves, slightly furry to the touch, are topped with clusters of small, soft violet-blue flowers. 60 cm (2 ft).

tabernaemontana salicifolia Open sprays of blue stars are carried on well-branched, black stems with pointed, shiny, grey-green leaves, similar to those of a citrus fruit tree. 90 cm (3 ft).

ANAPHALIS (Pearl Everlasting)

This, like all grey foliage plants, is very useful for binding a wide variety of colours together. They produce low mounds of soft, spear-shaped leaves, and later, sprays of rather insignificant papery flowers. Grow in a well-drained soil that does not dry out, in sun or partial shade. Summer.

margaritacea yedoensis Well-behaved, round mounds of spear-shaped leaves, coated with white hairs, bear terminal clusters of small, round, paper-white flowers. AGM. 75 cm (2½ft).

nepalensis monocephala This forms compact, low, spreading mounds with pointed, grey-green leaves that are soft to the touch. It bears small, round, yellow flowers each surrounded by papery bracts and is ideal for the front of a border. 30 cm (1 ft).

Anaphalis margaritacea yedoensis

Anaphalis nepalensis monocephala

Anchusa azurea 'Dropmore'　　*Anchusa azurea 'Loddon Royalist'*

Anchusa azurea 'Opal'

Anemone 'Bressingham Glow'

Anemone 'Hadspen Abundance'

Anemone 'Prinz Heinrich'

Anemone hupehensis 'September Charm'

ANCHUSA (Bugloss)

An upright plant, similar in habit to a delphinium, with small, single, truly blue flowers. The stems are tall, thick, distinctly hairy and sparsely clothed with long, rough leaves. Unfortunately, these can be temperamental to grow unless provided with a deep, rich, moist soil in sun or partial shade. Summer.

azurea **'Dropmore'** Small, vivid deep blue flowers. 90 cm (3 ft).

azurea **'Loddon Royalist'** Small, rich purple-blue flowers. AGM. 90 cm (3 ft).

azurea **'Opal'** Large, soft blue flowers, more sapphire than opal, with mahogany-red stems. 90 cm (3 ft).

ANEMONE
(Japanese Anemone)

These must be the epitome of elegance in the late summer and autumn garden. Their simple, open flowers are carried on tall, silky, well-branched stems above a clump of vine-shaped leaves. They are ideal for mixed borders, even ones along dry, warm walls; once established, these tolerant plants can be left untouched for years. Plant in a humus-rich, well-drained soil, in sun or partial shade. Late summer into autumn.

'Bressingham Glow' Whirling rosettes of semi-double, rich rose-pink flowers. 90 cm (3 ft).

'Hadspen Abundance' A single, deep pink flower, oval in shape and paler in colour around the edges. AGM. 75 cm (2½ft).

'Prinz Heinrich' Very dark rose-pink, almost double flowers, with uneven petals. AGM. 105 cm (3½ft).

hupehensis **'September Charm'** A classic Japanese anemone. Soft, clear pink cups with darker backs to the petals. Very free flowering. AGM. 105 cm (3½ft).

Anemone x hybrida 'Honorine Jobert'

Anemone x hybrida 'Königin Charlotte'

x hybrida **'Honorine Jobert'** One of the most reliable varieties with glowing white petals and golden stamens. It is often listed under *A.* x *hybrida* 'Alba'.
AGM. 105 cm (3½ft).

x hybrida **'Königin Charlotte'** Perfectly shaped soft pink flowers.
AGM. 120 cm (4 ft).

x hybrida **'Monterosa'** A semi-double, soft pink flower with many neatly crumpled petals around a centre of small stamens. It may need staking. 120 cm (4 ft).

x hybrida **'Pamina'** A mass of small, rich deep pink, semi-double flowers, like rosettes, are borne on well-branched, dark brown stems. A free-flowering and compact plant. 90 cm (3 ft).

ANTHEMIS (Chamomile)

These pretty plants, related to the herbal chamomiles, carry a joyous air about them. A lush mound of highly fragrant, deeply cut foliage is covered throughout the summer with great quantities of single, daisy-shaped flowers. They make wonderful border specimens for 'cottagey' gardens, although they are short-lived, especially in rich soil. Take cuttings each year, or be prepared to renew them every two or three years. Plant in any well-drained soil, in sun or partial shade. Summer.

punctata cupaniana A low, spreading mound of silver foliage pours forth a profusion of daisies for weeks on end. It needs a well-drained, sunny site, such as the edge of a low wall. AGM. 30 cm (1 ft).

tinctoria **'E.C. Buxton'** A profusion of light lemon flowers is borne above a mound of rich green foliage. 60 cm (2 ft).

Anemone x hybrida 'Monterosa'

Anemone x hybrida 'Pamina'   *Anemone punctata cupaniana*

Anthemis tinctoria 'E.C. Buxton'

tinctoria **'Grallagh Gold'** Similar in theme to all the other *A. tinctoria* types, but with large flowers of golden yellow and deep green foliage. 60 cm (2 ft).

tinctoria **'Sauce Hollandaise'** Large cream flowers, the petals curling back and paling with age to almost white. Dark green foliage. 60 cm (2 ft).

tinctoria **'Wargrave'** A sea of soft cream daisies with large, golden centres and deep green foliage. 60 cm (2 ft).

ANTHRISCUS *sylvestris* **'Ravenswing'** (Black Cow Parsley, Queen Anne's Lace)

So many of the most recently introduced plants are selections of our common European wild flowers, just as this one is. This forms a frothy sea of white, with lacy umbels of tiny flowers and dark brown stems above lush mounds of deeply divided, parsley-shaped foliage. It is a biennial, or a short-lived perennial, for wild plantings and less formal borders, which needs to be allowed to self-seed. Grow in any well-drained soil, in sun or partial shade. Early summer. 120 cm (4 ft).

ANTIRRHINUM *braun-blanquettii* (Perennial Snapdragon)

Spikes of soft lemon and white flowers, shaped like the muzzle of a dragon, are surrounded by pointed, soft green leaves to form a low, spreading clump. It flowers for weeks and is ideal for filling borders quickly, but as it is rather short lived, allow it to set seed. Grow in a well-drained soil, in sun. Summer. 45 cm (18 in).

Anthriscus sylvestris 'Ravenswing'

Anthemis tinctoria 'Sauce Hollandaise'

Anthemis tinctoria 'Wargrave'

Anthemis tinctoria 'Grallagh Gold'

Antirrhinum braun-blanquettii

Aquilegia vulgaris

Aquilegia alpina

Aquilegia 'McKana's' hybrids

AQUILEGIA (Columbine)

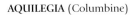

These are the very essence of the English 'Cottage Garden'. Each nodding, bell-shaped flower is covered by a cap of pointed petals. These extend backwards into long, thin tubes referred to as 'spurs'. The flowers are carried with dignity on tall, slender, well-branched stems above whorls of round, shallowly cut, glaucous leaves. They will liberally self-seed, hence the wide selection of colours and forms available. Grow in a well-drained soil that does not dry out, in sun or dappled shade. Late spring into summer.

Aquilegia vulgaris alba

alpina Hardly a plant of 'alpine' proportions as it bears large, rich navy blue flowers on tall, upright stems. 75 cm (2½ft).

'McKana's' hybrids This produces very large blooms with long spurs, that trail behind the flower like the dangling legs of some harmless insect. While the colours vary, the flowers are always in two soft tones, such as lemon or pastel pink. 90 cm (3 ft).

vulgaris (Granny's Bonnet) My favourite *Aquilegia* with masses of neatly formed, short-spurred bells. These days they can be purchased under a variety of titles that refer to the colour, but they are generally found in shades of rich blue, purple or mauve. 90 cm (3 ft).

vulgaris alba A pure white form of *A. vulgaris* with pale green foliage. 90 cm (3 ft).

vulgaris flore-pleno Round, ball-like flowers filled with many pointed petals, in shades of rich blue, purple and sometimes white or pink. The foliage is mid-green. 90 cm (3 ft).

vulgaris **'Nora Barlow'** This rather inelegant plant is somewhat of a curiosity. It produces small, round, frilly flowers that are made up of many pale green petals, each tinted with red. AGM. 90 cm (3 ft).

vulgaris **'William Guiness'** Deep purple, short-spurred flowers with a centre of white petals that deepen to purple at the base. Also known as 'Magpie', the seedling may turn out to be pure black. 90 cm (3 ft).

Aquilegia vulgaris flore-pleno

Aquilegia vulgaris 'Nora Barlow'

Aquilegia vulgaris 'William Guiness'

Armoracia rusticana 'Variegata'

Artemisia lactiflora 'Guizhou'

Artemisia pontica

Artemesia stelleriana

Artemesia absinthium 'Lambrook Mist'

Artemisia ludoviciana 'Valerie Finnis'

ARMORACIA *rusticana* **'Variegata'** (Variegated Horseradish)

This indestructible plant produces a very handsome clump of long, upright, wavy leaves, beautifully mottled and streaked with cream. It throws up tall stems with panicles of tiny, white flowers. Beware, it needs to be placed carefully as, once established, nothing short of a JCB will remove its deep roots. Grow in any well-drained soil, in sun. Summer. 90 cm (3 ft).

ARTEMISIA (Wormwood)

A family of useful grey-foliaged plants with spikes of tiny white flowers that add little to the plant's personality. It is ideal for growing in borders with other softly coloured plants and nicely complements shrub roses. As they are mainly from warm, dry areas of the Mediterranean, they prefer to be grown in a sunny position, in well-drained soil.

absinthium **'Lambrook Mist'** Deeply divided, grey-green leaves form a lacy clump with upright stems carrying tiny, silver flowers. Summer. 90 cm (3 ft).

lactiflora **'Guizhou'** Unusual amongst the artemisias, as this is not silver. I suspect that we will find it reclassified by botanists in a few years' time. Upright stems are covered with deeply divided dark maroon leaves and topped with open spikes of tiny, budlike, white flowers. It needs a moist soil in sun or partial shade. Late summer. 150 cm (5 ft).

ludoviciana **'Valerie Finnis'** A pewter-grey plant. Smooth, pointed leaves grow into a tumbling mass and produce small spikes of tiny, silver flowers. It mixes well with rich purple flowers. AGM. Summer. 60 cm (2 ft).

pontica (Roman Wormwood) A soft cushion of tiny, lacy, grey leaves sends up slender, upright stems of little grey flowers. This is a perfect plant for edging and for smaller borders. AGM. Summer. 45 cm (18 in).

stelleriana A low, spreading plant with chrysanthemum-shaped, silver leaves that are velvety to the touch. These produce arching sprays of tiny, yellow flowers. Summer. 30 cm (1 ft).

ARUNCUS *dioicus* (Goat's Beard)

One of those plants, like pampas grass, that is often found taking pride of place in borders at the front of a house. It produces a large clump of broad, deeply divided mid-green leaves and wispy spires of tiny, cream flowers. Grow in any soil, well-drained or moist, in sun or light shade. Summer. 180 cm (6 ft).

ASPHODELINE (Jacob's Rod)

This produces erect stems with handsome pokers of starry flowers above whorls of slender, grasslike, grey-green leaves. The flowers open in an uneven manner to form an unusual plant that originates from drier regions of the Mediterranean. It is ideal for rocky areas and sandy soil, in sun. Late spring into summer.

liburnica A delicate, yet tough plant, with slender stems of yellow flowers that open during the afternoon and last only a day. However, there are many more flowers to follow. 60 cm (2 ft).

lutea (King's Spear, Yellow Asphodel) A robust plant with bright yellow flowers carried on strong stems. This is useful for large planting schemes. 90 cm (3 ft).

ASTER

Think of an autumn garden and I dare you not to include asters. These robust plants bear colourful, daisy-shaped flowers predominantly in shades of lilac-blue, pink or white. They are indispensable for late-flowering borders, providing colour when so many other plants are preparing to go to bed for the winter. However, it is a large family with hidden depth and a lot to offer. I like to grow varying types close together, as each variety will enhance the one near to it. Grow in any fertile, well-drained soil, in sun.

amellus hybrids

These non-invasive and disease-resistant plants are of European origin. They produce low, broad clumps with soft foliage and large flowers. Unfortunately, when heavily in bloom the stems tend to flop forward. Don't be put off, as a little discreet staking will solve the problem. Late summer into autumn.

amellus **'Brilliant'** Deep lilac-pink flowers. 60 cm (2 ft).

amellus **'King George'** Large, rich violet-blue flowers. AGM. 60 cm (2 ft).

Aruncus dioicius

Asphodeline liburnica

Asphodeline lutea

Aster amellus 'King George'

Aster amellus 'Brilliant'

Aster amellus 'Rosa Erfüllung'

Aster amellus 'Veilchenkönigin'

Aster amellus 'Rudolph Goethe'

amellus **'Rosa Erfüllung'** Soft mauve-pink flowers. 60 cm (2 ft).

amellus **'Rudolph Goethe'** Large flowers of pure violet. 75 cm (2½ft).

amellus **'Sonia'** Delicate sprays of small, lilac-pink flowers that fade in colour towards the centre. 45 cm (18 in).

amellus **'Veilchenkönigin'** Delicately formed flowers of pure violet. AGM. 45 cm (18 in).

'Coombe Fishacre' An old variety that forms an upright dome, smothered with small, pale lilac flowers. The fluffy centres start soft yellow and gradually become soft maroon. AGM. Mid autumn. 90 cm (3 ft).

divaricatus Clouds of white flowers on black stems with pointed, oval leaves. Early autumn. 45 cm (18 in).

Aster amellus 'Sonia'

Aster divaricatus

Aster 'Coombe Fishacre'

ericoides hybrids

A network of fine, wiry stems with small, slender leaves forms a round clump that is literally smothered with hundreds of very small daisies. These are a lovely group of late-flowered asters with a short but sweet flowering period. Early to late autumn.

ericoides 'Cinderella' Spiky mounds covered with tiny, white daisies. 45 cm (18 in).

ericoides 'Erlkönig' An airy plant smothered with pale violet flowers. 90 cm (3 ft).

ericoides 'Pink Cloud' Tiny, soft lilac-pink flowers. AGM. 105 cm (3½ ft).

ericoides 'Ring Dove' A waterfall of tiny, grey-pink flowers each with a large, maroon centre. It sounds rather mournful colour wise, but it is very pretty. 90 cm (3 ft).

x frikartii 'Mönch' Large, deep lilac flowers. A most useful plant for late summer borders. AGM. Late summer into autumn. 60 cm (2 ft).

lateriflorus 'Prince' Little white flowers cover a compact mound of maroon foliage for weeks. It is one of the last asters to flower, lasting well into November. 60 cm (2 ft).

'Little Carlow' An upright bush with large, pointed leaves covered with masses of bright mid-blue flowers, veering in colour towards violet. AGM. Mid autumn. 90 cm (3 ft).

Aster ericoides 'Cinderella'

Aster ericoides 'Erlkönig'

Aster ericoides 'Pink Cloud'

Aster ericoides 'Ring Dove'

Aster x frikartii 'Mönch'

Aster lateriflorus 'Prince'

Aster 'Little Carlow'

Aster novae-angliae 'Barr's Blue'

Aster novae-angliae 'Barr's Pink'

Aster novae-angliae 'Harrington's Pink'

Aster novae-angliae 'Andenken an Alma Pötschke'

novae-angliae hybrids (New England Aster)

An upright plant with soft green, disease-resistant leaves topped by clusters of fairly large flowers. The tall varieties are ideal for the back of a border and look lovely if planted behind smaller, more delicate types such as the *A. ericoides* hybrids. These trouble-free plants, being greedy feeders, need frequent splitting and a soil that does not dry out, in sun or partial shade. Autumn.

novae-angliae **'Andenken an Alma Pötschke'** Single, rich cerise-pink flowers with orange centres. AGM. 120 cm (4 ft).

novae-angliae **'Barr's Blue'** Deep violet-blue flowers with bronze centres. 105 cm (3½ ft).

Aster novae-angliae 'Herbstschnee'

novae-angliae **'Barr's Pink'** Single, violet-pink flowers with orange centres. 120 cm (4 ft).

novae-angliae **'Harrington's Pink'** Flowers of softest baby-pink, one of the purest pink asters. AGM. 150 cm (5 ft).

novae-angliae **'Herbstschnee'** Pure white flowers held in tight bunches. AGM. 120 cm (4 ft).

novae-angliae **'Purple Dome'** Very short, dense growth that is upright and domed at the top. This is covered with bronze-centred, truly purple flowers. Late blooming. 30 cm (1 ft).

Aster novae-angliae 'Purple Dome'

Aster novi-belgii 'Audrey'

Aster novi-belgii 'Blandie'

Aster novi-belgii 'Boningale White'

Aster novi-belgii 'Chequers'

Aster novi-belgii 'Fellowship'

***novi-belgii* hybrids** (Michaelmas Daisies)
The shiny leaves of these much hybridised
asters are famously prone to attacks of
mildew, which is a great pity, as their
vibrant colours add so much to autumn
borders. However, the problem can be
lessened by spraying regularly with a
fungicide and providing the right growing
conditions. Plant in an open site with rich
moist soil. Autumn.

novi-belgii **'Audrey'** Bright lilac-blue flowers
cover a dense dome of leaves. 30 cm (1 ft).

novi-belgii **'Blandie'** Creamy white flowers
with tall stems of bright green leaves. 120
cm (4 ft).

novi-belgii **'Boningale White'** Clusters of
white flowers. 105 cm (3½ft).

novi-belgii **'Chequers'** Large sprays of semi-
double, violet flowers. 75 cm (2½ft).

novi-belgii **'Fellowship'** Large, loose, semi-
double, soft lilac-pink flowers. 90 cm (3 ft).

novi-belgii **'Jenny'** A low mound of foliage
is covered with semi-double, vivid carmine
flowers. 45 cm (18 in).

Aster novi-belgii 'Jenny'

Aster novi-belgii 'Little Pink Beauty'

Aster novi-belgii 'Lady in Blue'

novi-belgii **'Lady in Blue'** Double, lilac-blue flowers are borne over a tight hummock of leaves. 30 cm (1 ft).

novi-belgii **'Little Pink Beauty'** A wide clump of foliage with single, mauve-pink flowers. 30 cm (1 ft).

novi-belgii **'Marie Ballard'** Neat, double, powder-blue flowers. This is perhaps the most blue of all asters. 105 cm ($3\frac{1}{2}$ ft).

novi-belgii **'Mistress Quickly'** Deep violet-purple flowers. 90 cm (3 ft).

novi-belgii **'Newton's Pink'** A low-growing variety with double flowers of soft pink. 45 cm (18 in).

novi-belgii **'Patricia Ballard'** Tidy growing, semi-double, rose-pink flowers. 90 cm (3 ft).

Aster novi-belgii 'Marie Ballard'

Aster novi-belgii 'Mistress Quickly'

Aster novi-belgii 'Newton's Pink'

Aster novi-belgii 'Patricia Ballard'

Aster novi-belgii 'Percy Thrower'

Aster novi-belgii 'Rose Bonnet'

Aster pringlei 'Monte Cassino'

novi-belgii **'Percy Thrower'** Heavy clusters of deep violet flowers, large and double. 90 cm (3 ft).

novi-belgii **'Rose Bonnet'** Dense mound of single, soft lilac-pink flowers. 45 cm (18 in).

pringlei **'Monte Cassino'** Delicate sprays of little white daisies are borne on airy, branched stems with almost fernlike, light green foliage. This is an excellent flower for cutting and is one of the last to bloom. Mid autumn. 60 cm (2 ft).

pyrenaeus **'Lutetia'** Large, single, lilac, daisy-shaped flowers smother a low, spreading clump of foliage. Mid autumn. 45 cm (18 in).

sedifolius Slim, grey-green leaves form a tumbling mass that is smothered with scented stars of pure lilac. Early autumn. 60 cm (2 ft).

Aster pyrenaeus 'Lutetia'

Aster sedifolius

Astilbe x arendsii 'Fanal'

Astilbe x arendsii 'Hyazinth'

Astilbe x arendsii 'Irrlicht'

Astilbe x arendsii 'Snowdrift'

Astilbe x arendsii 'Venus'

Astilbe chinenis taquetii 'Purpurlanze'

Astilbe thunbergii 'Betsy Cuperus'

Astilbe thunbergii 'Straussenfeder'

ASTILBE

In 1957 Frances Perry stated that astilbes 'occupy an important place in late planting schemes'. I cannot share this view but it does illustrate how plants come in and out of fashion. These handsome plants form round clumps with deeply divided foliage and slender stems of tiny, fluffy flowers. Traditionally, they are used around the edges of ponds, where, if placed in large groups, can look very effective. They need to be grown in a rich, very moist soil, which may account for their decline in popularity, since our summers have become warmer and drier. However, there are varieties that will survive quite a degree of dryness. Grow in partial or full shade. Midsummer.

x arendsii **'Fanal'** Short panicles of wine-red flowers with compact foliage. AGM. 60 cm (2 ft).

x arendsii **'Hyazinth'** Rosy pink flowers borne in dense panicles. 90 cm (3 ft).

x arendsii **'Irrlicht'** Very pale pink flowers form broad, fluffy spikes. 60 cm (2 ft).

x arendsii **'Snowdrift'** Compact, light green foliage with short fat panicles of creamy white flowers. 45 cm (18 in).

x arendsii **'Venus'** Open spikes of soft, silvery pink flowers. 75 cm (2½ ft).

chinenis taquetii **'Purpurlanze'** Slender spikes of rosy purple flowers with deep green foliage. 120 cm (4 ft).

thunbergii **'Betsy Cuperus'** Long, arching, pink stems with panicles of softest pink flowers. 90 cm (3 ft).

thunbergii **'Straussenfeder'** Arching stems of salmon-pink flowers. AGM. 90 cm (3 ft).

thunbergii **'Professor van der Wielen'** Sprays of tiny, white flowers. This will grow well in drier soils. Late to flower. 90 cm (3 ft).

Astilbe thunbergii 'Professor van der Wielen'

ASTRANTIA (Masterwort)

Astrantias are one of my favourite perennials. They are not showy but deserve pride of place in any border because of their uniquely formed flowers. These look like posies wrapped in laced handkerchiefs. Each bloom is made up of a dome of thin, tubular flowers seated on a ring of pointed bracts. They are carried in sprays, on wiry, well-branched stems above a clump of deeply cut leaves. Cut back after flowering to encourage more flowers. They are suitable for both shady sites and sunnier borders with a well-drained soil that remains moist. Summer.

major Paper-like, fresh white flowers appear from red tinted buds. A variety that will seed itself around. 90 cm (3 ft).

major 'Canneman' This may not be the most available of astrantias, but I think it is one the best. A low-growing plant with richly tinted red-green foliage produces stems of large, rosy pink flowers. 75 cm (2½ ft).

major 'Hadspen Blood' Large clusters of rich wine-red flowers are borne well above mounds of richly coloured red-green leaves. 105 cm (3½ ft).

major involucrata 'Shaggy' This produces large white flowers with pointed, green tipped bracts. AGM. 90 cm (3 ft).

major rosea Red-pink flowers with a tint of green at the base of each bract. Beware, some of the plants available commercially are grown from seed and are therefore variable in colour. 90 cm (3 ft).

major rubra Ruby-red bracts with soft red flowers, green at the base, are carried on red stems above mounds of dark green leaves. 75 cm (2½ ft).

major 'Sunningdale Variegated' Small, green-white flowers with pink tinted bracts are borne above light green leaves. These are dramatically splashed with cream and later in the year turn green. A variety that is slow to multiply. AGM. 90 cm (3 ft).

maxima Dusky pink flowers, that bear their pollen like a dusting of white icing, are borne above starry, pink bracts. AGM. 75 cm (2½ ft).

Astrantia major

Astrantia major 'Canneman'

Astrantia major 'Hadspen Blood'

Astrantia major involucrata 'Shaggy'

Astrantia major rosea

Astrantia major rubra

Astrantia major 'Sunningdale Variegated'

Astrantia maxima

Athyrium felix-femina 'Frizelliae'

Baptisia australis

Athyrium niponicum pictum

ATHYRIUM

A group of deciduous ferns that like moist, shady places such as light woodland and hillside gardens. They are extremely easy to grow and combine well with other shade-loving plants such as hostas.

felix-femina **'Frizelliae'** (Mrs. Frizell's Lady Fern) This has large, triangular, deeply divided, light green leaves. It slowly evolves into a handsome, upright clump. AGM. 30 cm (1 ft).

niponicum pictum (Painted Fern) A prostrate plant and one of the most beautiful for foliage. It produces triangular, deeply divided, silver-green leaves that, in a dark spot, seem to glisten when light hits them. AGM. 30 cm (1 ft).

BAPTISIA *australis* (False Indigo)

A distinctly blue plant that produces a thick, dense, round and upright clump with long stems of blue-green leaves, like those of the pea plant. These end in short, open spikes of small, lupin-like flowers. It is a slowly spreading plant, ideal for a dry or well-drained soil, in sun. Summer. 120 cm (4 ft).

BARBAREA *vulgaris* **'Variegata'** (St. Barbara's Herb)

A variegated foliage plant for placing along the edge of borders. Its deep green leaves, splashed unevenly with cream, form loose rosettes from which short, well-branched spikes of tiny, yellow, cross-shaped flowers appear. A short-lived evergreen plant that readily seeds itself around. Grow in a well-drained soil, in sun or partial shade. Early summer. 30 cm (1 ft).

Barbarea vulgaris 'Variegata'

Bergenia 'Abendglut'

Bergenia 'Baby Doll'

BERGENIA
(Elephant's Ears)

Not the most diverse or perhaps the most exciting of plants, but essential for their evergreen foliage and spring flowers. They form a bold, slowly spreading clump of large, leathery leaves. From these emerge thick, stout stems bearing clusters of bell-shaped flowers in shades of pink and white. If the autumn or winter is cold enough, and there have been sharp frosts, the foliage will take on hues of red and bronze. They can be included in borders, under shrubs, on the edges of walls – almost any situation. Once established, they are almost indestructible, living for years without division. Plant in any well-drained soil, in sun or shade. Early to mid spring.

'**Abendglut**' Bright pink flowers that are unusual because they are semi-double and slightly frilled. The foliage is round and not totally frost-resistant. 23 cm (9 in).

'**Baby Doll**' Heavy clusters of soft pink bells are carried above upright, round, deep green leaves. In winter the leaves gain a red tint and can sometimes be damaged by frost. 30 cm (1 ft).

'**Ballawley**' Tight clusters of magenta bells are carried above a clump of leaves. The leaves are as large as those of a cabbage, uneven, slightly shiny, oval and rich green. AGM. 60 cm (2 ft).

'**Beethoven**' Large heads of white flowers, flushed with pink as they age, are carried above long, spoon-shaped, mid-green foliage. 30 cm (1 ft).

Bergenia 'Ballawley'

Bergenia 'Beethoven'

Bergenia 'Bressingham White'

Bergenia cordifolia

Bergenia 'Oeschberg'

Bergenia 'Silberlicht'

Bergenia 'Sunningdale'

Bergenia 'Wintermärchen'

'Bressingham White' Pure white flowers borne in clusters are produced on neatly arched stems. The long, spoon-shaped foliage is vigorous, broad and deep green with a finely toothed edge. In winter it gains tints of red-brown. AGM. 45 cm (18 in).

cordifolia An old, reliable variety from Russia that produces open clumps of large, round, matt green leaves. These are deeply veined, undulating, notched along the edges and in winter, heavily tinted with red. The flowers are lilac-pink, trumpet-shaped and borne in loose sprays on red-tinted stems. 60 cm (2 ft).

'Oeschberg' Although not readily available, this is one of the finest varieties for winter colour. It produces long, oval leaves that curl at the edges with tight clusters of bright pink, tubular flowers, white at the base. By early spring, the shiny leaves are a smooth, pure red. 60 cm (2 ft).

'Silberlicht' A late-flowering variety with white flowers produced on low stems. These become tinged with pink as they age. Here in the Midlands, this can be rather a disappointing plant as it is often damaged by frosts. It needs to be grown well to perform at its best. AGM. 30 cm (1 ft).

'Sunningdale' Bright pink, open trumpets are held in dense clusters above round, red-edged leaves that neatly curl back. This variety flowers again during the summer. AGM. 45 cm (18 in).

'Wintermärchen' A tight clump is formed with slender, oval, shiny leaves that become mahogany-red in winter. It carries drooping clusters of pink flowers on long, slightly furry stems, just above its leaves. 30 cm (1 ft).

BOLTONIA *asteroides*

A very upright, late-flowering perennial that is suitable for the back of a border or wild areas. Loose clusters of small, white, daisy-shaped flowers are borne on tall stems with slim, grey-green foliage. It suits a sunny site and a soil that does not dry out during the summer. Autumn. 180 cm (6 ft).

BRIZA *media* (Quaking Grass)

A neat and good-tempered plant that does not spread. Slim, mid-green leaves form a neat clump and produce loose, airy sprays of tiny, red-tinted, oat-shaped flowers. Grow in any well-drained soil, in sun or partial shade. Summer. 60 cm (2 ft).

BRUNNERA

These are plants that I cannot get terribly excited about, perhaps because in spring there are so many blue-flowering alternatives. They produce airy sprays of small, Forget-Me-Not-like flowers for weeks on end above a dense clump of large, heart-shaped leaves. These are useful for a moist border or lightly shaded area, such as woodland, where they can be used for ground cover. However, the variegated forms are not as robust and tend to be expensive. If they revert, as most variegated plants do, make sure the plain green leaves are removed. Spring.

macrophylla A round clump of roughly textured, heart-shaped, mid-green leaves is smothered with bright blue flowers and borne on slender, well-branched stems. AGM. 45 cm (18 in).

macrophylla 'Dawson's White' This produces the same blue flowers as its sister, but the leaves are distinctively splashed with white. 45 cm (18 in).

macrophylla 'Hadspen Cream' The mid-green leaves are marked with a narrow band of cream. Its flowers are mid-blue. AGM. 45 cm (18 in).

BUPHTHALMUM *salicifolium*

A joyful, undisciplined plant that produces a mass of golden yellow daisies. These are carried individually on upright stems above somewhat unruly, dark green leaves. Unlike many daisy-flowered perennials, it is not harsh and, as it freely seeds itself around, is best used in informal borders. Grow in any well-drained soil, in sun. Midsummer. 75 cm (2½ft).

Boltonia asteroides

Briza media

Brunnera macrophylla

Brunnera macrophylla 'Dawson's White'

Brunnera macrophylla 'Hadspen Cream'

Buphthalmum salicifolium

Calamintha grandiflora

Calamintha nepeta 'White Cloud'

Calamintha nepeta 'Blue Cloud'

Calamintha nepeta

CALAMINTHA (Calamint)

Charming plants that are rather deferential in appearance but perfect for the front of a border. A round clump is formed from small, mint-scented leaves and covered for weeks with spikes of small, tubular flowers, that quietly encourage bees and butterflies. They will seed themselves around and grow well in a very well-drained soil, in sun. Mid to late summer.

grandiflora Leafy spikes of large, lilac-pink flowers are carried on upright stems which gradually spread to form a lush, round clump. Whereas the other members of this family are suitable for the front of a border, this one can be used in the middle. 45 cm (18 in).

nepeta Tiny, soft pink flowers nestle amongst a compact and tidy mound of small, round, shiny leaves. 30 cm (1 ft).

nepeta **'Blue Cloud'** Small, lilac-blue flowers with soft green leaves and stems, tinted steely blue, forming a misty haze. 30 cm (1 ft).

nepeta **'White Cloud'** A small, very white plant with soft, mid-green leaves and lots of purest white flowers. 30 cm (1 ft).

Caltha palustris

Caltha palustris 'Flore Pleno'

CALTHA (Marsh Marigold, Kingcup)

These are delightful plants for lighting up the edges of shallow ponds. Dense clumps of round, shiny, deep green foliage throw up short, branched stems of golden flowers. Plant in any boggy soil or at the extreme edges of ponds, in sun or partial shade. Spring.

palustris Single, golden-yellow, buttercup-like flowers. AGM. 45 cm (18 in).

palustris 'Flore Pleno' Tight, double flowers of bright yellow. AGM. 30 cm (1 ft).

CAMASSIA *leichtlinii* (Quamash)

These bulbous perennials are found in the meadowlands of North America. They produce upright stems with broad spires of starry, soft blue flowers. Like many bulbs, they will die back after flowering, but these are excellent for naturalising in long grass and for growing in mixed borders. Grow in any very well-drained soil, in sun or partial shade. AGM. Summer. 90 cm (3 ft).

CAMPANULA
(Bellflower)

These are some of the easiest plants to grow and use in a mixed border. All the members of this large family produce bell-shaped flowers in shades of white, pink and blue. They blend beautifully with the majority of herbaceous perennials and many shrubs, including old roses. These are most definitely 'flowery' plants, gentle by design but not by nature. They grow in one of two ways. The taller types grow from a central crown, which means they are upright and tend not to spread. However, the smaller kinds tend to be spreading by nature and need to be placed carefully as they can become invasive. All varieties thrive in any well-drained soil, in sun or partial shade. Unless stated they are generally summer-flowering.

alliariifolia Small, milk-white bells are carried on short, upright stems with soft, velvety textured, pale green, triangular leaves forming a neat clump. This is sometimes sold as C. 'Ivory Bells'. Midsummer to early autumn. 45 cm (18 in).

'Burghaltii' Dangling, soft lilac and tubular bell-like hats, emerge from long, purple buds above broad, heart-shaped leaves that are serrated around the edges. A cross between *C. latifolia* and *C. punctata*, which may need staking. AGM. 60 cm (2 ft).

Camassia leichtlinii

Campanula alliariifolia

Campanula 'Burghaltii'

Campanula 'Elizabeth'

Campanula glomerata 'Superba'

Campanula glomerata alba

Campanula 'Kent Belle'

'Elizabeth' A selection from the *C. takesimana* tribe with long bells of deep maroon, marked with dark spots inside. Heart-shaped leaves form rosettes that grow into a slowly creeping carpet. AGM. 45 cm (18 in).

glomerata alba Whorls of pure white, upright bells form clusters on short, leafy stems. A perennial for the front of a border, which is effective when planted in drifts. 45 cm (18 in).

glomerata **'Superba'** A spreading clump of red stems topped with tight clusters of deep violet bells and surrounded by light green foliage. Front of the border plant. AGM. 60 cm (2 ft).

'Kent Belle' A useful plant for its intense colour. Long bells of deep purple are carried on long stems. Like many of this type (*C. Burghaltii*, *C.* 'Elizabeth' and *C. punctata* included), its spreading growth produces low, heart-shaped leaves that wander about the border with enthusiasm. 75 cm (2½ ft).

lactiflora (Milk Bellflower) Tall stems with heart-shaped, light green leaves, are thrown up from a central crown and topped with rounded clusters of small, open, soft blue bells. These often vary in colour, as it is usually produced from seed. The *C. lactiflora* varieties grow into the largest plants and are ideal for bigger borders. 150 cm (5 ft).

Campanula lactiflora

Campanula lactiflora 'Alba'

Campanula lactiflora 'Loddon Anna'

Campanula lactiflora 'Pritchard's Variety'

Campanula latifolia alba

Campanula latifolia

Campanula latiloba 'Alba'

Campanula latiloba 'Hidcote Amethyst'

lactiflora **'Alba'** Soft white flowers, sometimes tinted with blue. 150 cm (5 ft).

lactiflora **'Loddon Anna'** I have seen this described as pink, but it is not – it produces flowers of very pale lilac. AGM. 150 cm (5 ft).

lactiflora **'Pritchard's Variety'** A richly coloured plant with billowing clusters of deep violet-blue flowers. AGM. 150 cm (5 ft).

latifolia A European native of meadows and open woodlands that forms handsome spires. It is very upright in habit with long, tubular, lilac-blue bells popping from each leaf node on strong, leafy stems. This will tolerate a good degree of shade. 120 cm (4 ft).

latifolia alba A white-flowered form of its lilac-blue sister. 120 cm (4 ft).

latiloba **'Alba'** A beautifully clean plant with openly cupped flowers of white carried on upright stems. AGM. 90 cm (3 ft).

latiloba **'Hidcote Amethyst'** Soft lilac, wide, bell-shaped flowers are borne on erect stems above evergreen foliage. AGM. 90 cm (3 ft).

Campanula latiloba 'Percy Piper'

Campanula latiloba 'Highcliffe Variety'

latiloba **'Highcliffe Variety'** Rich violet-blue flowers. AGM. 90 cm (3 ft).

latiloba **'Percy Piper'** Upright stems are thickly and closely covered with large, open flowers of lavender and held above rosettes of slim, deep green leaves. AGM. 90 cm (3 ft).

persicifolia (Peach-leaved Bellflower) Large, cupped, mid-blue flowers nod slightly on slender stems above rosettes of slim, shiny, light green leaves. It tends to be cultivated from seed, so the flower colour will vary. 90 cm (3 ft).

persicifolia alba This produces white bells, like the blue version. 90 cm (3 ft).

persicifolia **'Alba Coronata'** A delightful white-flowered variation. Each bloom produces an inner ring of petals to make it double. 75 cm (2½ ft).

Campanula persicifolia alba

persicifolia **'Chettle Charm'** A delicate, appropriately named plant with open bells of white, very neatly edged with a wash of lilac. 75 cm (2½ ft).

Campanula persicifolia

Campanula persicifolia 'Alba Coronata'

Campanula persicifolia 'Chettle Charm'

Campanula persicifolia 'Wortham Belle'

persicifolia 'Wortham Belle' Double flowers of rich blue are carried in profusion on upright stems. This was introduced by Howard & Kooij, a wholesale nursery based in Norfolk. 75 cm (2½ ft).

punctata A creeping variety with heart-shaped, mid-green leaves that form a dense carpet. From this brown stems erupt, bearing corrugated buds that open into long, dangling flowers of soft mauve, dotted inside with purple – although you have to lie on the ground to see this! Good in sandy soils. 30 cm (1 ft).

pyramidalis alba A beautiful plant with tall, very erect stems of cup-shaped, white flowers and light green leaves. Sadly, it can suffer in cold winters. 180 cm (6 ft).

sarmatica A low-growing plant with dangling, soft lilac-blue flowers, the edges curling upwards. 30 cm (1 ft).

takesimana Long, cap-shaped, white flowers are borne above spreading mid-green foliage. Each flower is spotted inside with maroon. 45 cm (18 in).

trachelium (Nettle-leaved Bellflower) This produces long, tubular bell-shaped, violet flowers that are held at 90 degrees to its leafy, upright stem. The edges to the petals are pointed and curl neatly outwards. The leaves are mid-green and deeply toothed at the edges. 90 cm (3 ft).

trachelium alba Very pure white flowers. 90 cm (3 ft).

trachelium 'Bernice' Tall, upright, leafy stems bear white buds that open into double, dark blue flowers. 90 cm (3 ft).

Campanula punctata

Campanula takesimana

Campanula trachelium alba

Campanula pyramidalis alba

Campanula sarmatica

Campanula trachelium

Campanula trachelium 'Bernice'

CAREX (Sedge)

Although not technically grasses, I have included the sedges within this group of plants. They are very similar and can be used in the same way. These two varieties will grow in a moist or wet area and can be planted along the edges of streams or ponds.

elata **'Aurea'** (Bowles' Golden Sedge) A very handsome plant that grows into a large clump with thin, golden leaves. These are finely edged with yellow and produce tight spikes of brown flowers. Early summer. 75 cm (2½ft).

pendula (Drooping Sedge) Long, broad, deep green leaves form a spreading clump and produce wands of slender, dangling flowers. This looks perfect along streams where the catkin-like flowers can droop poetically. 90 cm (3 ft).

CARLINA *acaulis* (Carline Thistle)

A highly decorative plant with large, flat, thistle-like flowers. These open at ground level, above long, prickly, mid-green leaves. The papery flowers have a large centre of bronze that is decorated around the edges with pointed, silver bracts. It is perfect for poor, stony, or hot soils, in sun. Late summer. 15 cm (6 in).

CATANACHE *caerulea* (Cupid's Dart)

This gentle plant is short-lived, but flowers for weeks on end. A sea of upright, slender stems carries, individually, lavender-blue flowers with papery, fringed petals. These emerge from a clump of narrow, grey-green leaves. It is an ideal plant for a sandy, well-drained soil, in sun, but will not thrive in a heavy soil. Summer. 60 cm (2 ft).

Carex elata 'Aurea'

Carlina acaulis

Catanache caerulea

Carex pendula

CENTAUREA (Knapweed)

These meadow plants are valuable for border plantings. Cornflower-like blooms are carried singly on long stems above long leaves. Some varieties will spread and become a menace, while others are well behaved and stay put. They prefer a soil that is not too rich and in sun. Late spring into summer.

dealbata **'Steenbergii'** Large, rich pink-lilac flowers are carried above a creeping clump of soft, fingered, grey-green foliage. This can be invasive. 45 cm (18 in).

hypoleuca **'John Coutts'** Slender, soft mauve flowers form a feathery ruff around a white centre. These are carried above a slowly spreading mound of mid-green leaves, white beneath. 45 cm (18 in).

macrocephala A distinctive and commanding plant that is good for flower arrangements. It produces large blooms that look like doorknobs. These are moulded from slim, deep yellow petals and are seated on a cone of brown bracts on upright, sturdy stems with long, mid-green leaves. 90 cm (3 ft).

montana Starry, violet-blue, cornflower-like blooms are held above a slowly spreading clump of long, silvery leaves. Tidy it up after the first flush of flowers to promote new growth and a second lot of flowers. Indestructible when planted in a soil that does not dry out. 45 cm (18 in).

montana alba A pure white form of *Centaurea montana*. 45 cm (18 in).

montana **'Parham'** Large flowers with soft lilac petals that form feathery swirls on long stems. 45 cm (18 in).

pulcherrima Small flowers of softest lilac with silver, deeply cut leaves. A small plant for the front of a border. 30 cm (1 ft).

'Pulchra Major' This is a handsome plant. It produces tight, lilac flowers that resemble the blooms of thistles. These are borne on a tiled mound of papery brown bracts above large, deeply dissected grey-green leaves. It is sometimes listed as *Leuzea centaureoides*. Midsummer. 90 cm (3 ft).

Centaurea dealbata 'Steenbergii'

Centaurea hypoleuca 'John Coutts'

Centaurea macrocephala

Centaurea montana

Centaurea montana alba

Centaurea montana 'Parham'

Centaurea pulcherrima

Centaurea 'Pulchra Major'

Centranthus ruber 'Albus'

Centranthus ruber coccineus

Cephalaria gigantea

CENTRANTHUS (Valerian)

A plant frequently seen growing between the stones of walls and on abandoned areas in south-western England. Its frothy, foaming heads are made up of tiny flowers that are carried on branched stems with long, pointed, light green leaves. It spreads freely by seed. Grow in any well-drained soil, in sun or partial shade. Summer.

ruber **'Albus'** White flowers. 60 cm (2 ft).

ruber coccineus Deep pink flowers. 60 cm (2 ft).

CEPHALARIA *gigantea* (Giant Scabious)

An impressive plant that needs a good deal of room but is marvellous for the back of a border or grown as a specimen plant. Clumps of deeply divided leaves give birth to very long, slender stems, topped with delicate, yellow scabious-type flowers. Plant in any well-drained soil in sun or partial shade. Summer. 180 cm (6 ft) and over.

CHAEROPHYLLUM *hirstum* **'Roseum'**

This is a decorative form of the herb chervil that produces a low mound of deeply split, soft green foliage. Above this grow short, branched stems holding lacy umbels of tiny, soft dusky pink flowers that pale to white with age. I'm sorry to say it, but this is loved by rabbits! Grow in a rich, moist soil in sun or partial shade. Early summer. 30 cm (1 ft).

CHELONE (Turtle's Head)

Clusters of tubular flowers are borne on upright stems and look remarkably like the faces of turtles staring into the sky. These form a slowly spreading clump with broad, pointed, mid-green leaves and are tolerant of almost all conditions including very wet and dry soils. Midsummer.

glabra Creamy white flowers. 75 cm (2½ ft).

obliqua Rich pink flowers. 60 cm (2 ft).

Chaerophyllum hirstum 'Roseum'

Chelone glabra

Chelone obliqua

Chrysanthemum rubellum 'Clara Curtis'

Chrysanthemum rubellum 'Emperor of China'

CHRYSANTHEMUM

The *Chrysanthemum* family is enormous and consists largely of plants grown for the commercial cut flower market. However, for the purposes of this book I have selected only the hybrids of *Chrysanthemum rubellum*. These I have found to be reliable garden varieties and, as they flower so very late in the season, invaluable border plants. They form broad, spreading clumps of mid-green leaves that, by mid autumn, are almost hidden by gently coloured, single, daisy-shaped flowers. They may require some staking and need dividing every two years to maintain their vigour. Otherwise, grow them in any well-drained soil, in sun or partial shade. Mid to late autumn.

rubellum **'Clara Curtis'** Cascading sprays of pure pink flowers. 75 cm (2½ft).

rubellum **'Emperor of China'** Large flowers of soft mauve-pink with a golden centre. 90 cm (3 ft).

rubellum **'Mary Stoker'** Soft apricot-yellow flowers. 75 cm (2½ft).

CICHORIUM (Chicory)

A decorative culinary perennial that produces very tall, upright, branched stems ending in flat, rosette-like flowers. The stems are sparsely covered with long, toothed, edible, mid-green leaves that can be added to salads. This is ideal for the back of a border, where it may need some staking. They will grow in any well-drained soil, poor or rich, in full or partial shade. If it sets seed, the offspring are always blue. Midsummer.

intybus album Purest white flowers. 150 cm (5 ft).

intybus **'Roseum'** Soft pink flowers. 150 cm (5 ft).

Cichorium intybus album

Cichorium intybus 'Roseum'

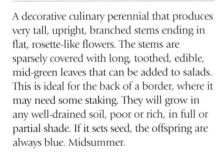

Chrysanthemum rubellum 'Mary Stoker'

Cimicifuga racemosa

Cimicifuga simplex 'White Pearl'

Cimicifuga simplex 'Atropurpurea'

Cimicifuga simplex 'Brunette'

CIMICIFUGA (Bugbane)

In autumn little can compare with these for elegance. They produce long wands of tiny flowers on tall, upright, slender stems. These are held well above an open clump of handsome, much-divided foliage. Although a little fussy about growing conditions, requiring a deep moist soil preferably in some shade, they need little attention once established. Late summer into autumn.

racemosa (Black Snake Root) A beautiful plant with fluffy spikes of white flowers on upright, branched stems with fresh green foliage. AGM. 180 cm (6 ft)

simplex **'White Pearl'** This is one of the easiest varieties to establish amongst these choice plants. Its erect pokers of white flowers are borne above mid-green foliage. 90 cm (3 ft).

simplex **'Atropurpurea'** White, furry pokers are made up of scented flowers that burst from mauve buds. These are borne on rich green-purple stems with dark maroon leaves. Above, the leaves possess a glaucous sheen; beneath, they are mint green. 180 cm (6 ft).

simplex **'Brunette'** Near black foliage and buds produce white flowers with stunning effect. Try planting this with vivid red plants such as *Monarda* 'Cambridge Scarlet'. 180 cm (6 ft).

CIRSIUM

Quietly elegant, short-lived perennials that are not commonly grown but are useful for adding height to a border. They require a very well-drained soil, in sun. Early to midsummer.

oleraceum Clean thistle-like heads of champagne-pink are tipped with deep rose-pink. These are carried on short stems and form an upright plant. 60 cm (2 ft).

rivulare **'Atropurpureum'** A plant with intense burgundy flowers. Small and flat on top, like thistles, they are borne on erect stems with a few long, mid-green leaves. 150 cm (5 ft).

Cirsium oleraceum

Cirsium rivulare 'Atropurpureum'

CLEMATIS

Herbaceous *Clematis* are the distinguished aristocrats of the perennial world, but they are not used enough. All the plants described here are non-clinging types with lax, sometimes rambling growth that will need some support. The flowering season can be short, but they will grow in any soil, in sun or partial shade.

'Arabella' A delicate plant with small, rosy purple flowers and long cream stamens. It is excellent for rambling through taller plants and, as far as I am aware, is a recent introduction. Late summer. 120 cm (4 ft).

x durandii This is a rambler with large, starry flowers of rich violet and a velvety texture. It is ideal for growing through early flowering shrubs. Summer. 180 cm (6 ft).

***heracleifolia* 'Côte d'Azur'** This is not really a rambler as it produces long, thick, almost clump-forming stems. From each leaf dense whorls of slightly scented, tubular, soft blue flowers appear, the rims of each petal peeling backwards. The leaves are very large, heart-shaped and mid-green. Autumn. 90 cm (3 ft).

recta Thick, leathery foliage of grey-green is borne on long, red-tinted stems. These terminate in heavy clusters of scented, milk-white stars, each with a centre of cream stamens. A variety that needs only a little support. Midsummer to late summer. 90 cm (3 ft).

***recta* 'Purpurea'** A highly valuable plant with richly tinted maroon foliage that perfectly compliments its creamy flowers. Midsummer to late summer. 120 cm (4 ft).

CONVALLARIA *majalis* (Lily-of-the-Valley)

The name 'Lily-of-the-valley' brings with it the suggestion of Christmas perfume and talcum powder. It produces extremely fragrant, white bells that dangle from arching stems amongst large, mid-green leaves. But don't be fooled by this demure plant, it is a territorial animal and once happily situated will take over, even pushing its way through tarmacked roads. Of course, this makes it excellent for ground covering despite its short but sweet flowering period. Grow in any soil, sun or shade. AGM. Late spring. 20 cm (9 in).

Clematis 'Arabella'

Clematis x durandii

Clematis heracleifolia 'Côte d'Azur'

Clematis recta

Clematis recta 'Purpurea'

Convallaria majalis

Coreopsis grandiflora 'Badengold'

Coreopsis 'Sunray'

Coreopsis verticillata

COREOPSIS (Tickseed)

These bright and breezy plants possess a gentle disposition. All produce bright yellow flowers on growth which is not over powering. They make good border plants, ideal for yellow or 'hot' planting schemes, and will grow in any well-drained soil, in sun. Mid to late summer.

grandiflora **'Badengold'** Long, bright green, wandering stems end in medium-sized, semi-double, truly yellow flowers with serrated edges to the petals. 90 cm (3 ft).

'Sunray' Large, double, glowing yellow flowers, buzzing with bees, are borne on short stems above long, mid-green leaves. A short-lived plant for high summer that never stops flowering. 75 cm (2½ft).

verticillata A profusion of starry, bright yellow flowers, neither large nor small, covers an intricate haze of wiry stems and small pointed foliage. It flowers for a long time. 60 cm (2 ft).

verticillata **'Moonbeam'** My favourite *Coreopsis* with rich lemon, starry flowers bursting above a mass of bronze-tinted stems and ferny foliage. It can take a while to reach peak performance. 45 cm (18 in).

CORTADERIA *selloana* (Pampas Grass)

This is probably one of the most commonly grown of ornamental grasses, other than those used for lawns! A handsome base is created from long, fine, mid-green leaves. Very upright, rigid stems appear above this, with dense, feathery plumes of long-lasting white flowers. These remain for months. A majestic plant, that will form a focal point in any garden. Plant in a well-drained soil, in sun. Late summer. 240 cm (8 ft).

COSMOS *atrosanguineus* (Chocolate Cosmos)

Just when you think that it has succumbed to the cold winter weather, this begins in early summer to sprout deep green, spatula-shaped leaves. Long, maroon stems of small, very dark maroon flowers are produced for weeks. These resemble velvety, miniature dahlias and are intriguingly scented of chocolate. A unique little plant, it forms low, round mounds and blends well with silver-leaved plants. It is of Mexican origin and therefore can be tender; however, we have few problems with it here in middle England. Plant in any well-drained soil, in sun. Late summer. 60 cm (2 ft).

Coreopsis verticillata 'Moonbeam'

Cortaderia selloana

Cosmos atrosanguineus

Crambe cordifolia

Crocosmia x crocosmiiflora

Crocosmia 'Emily McKenzie'

Crocosmia 'Golden Fleece'

Crocosmia 'James Coey'

Crocosmia 'Lucifer'

Crocosmia 'Mars'

CRAMBE *cordifolia*

Walk into a garden where this handsome plant is growing and it is not the immense size that strikes you, it's the scent. This produces large, loose sprays of white flowers, almost like *Gypsophila*, which exude a strong fragrance of honey. Underneath, the large, rough, dark green leaves form a good mound. Grow in any well-drained soil, including drier ones, in sun or partial shade. AGM. Midsummer. 180 cm (6 ft).

CROCOSMIA (Montbretia)

These are excellent plants for adding warm colour to a late summer border. A thick clump of slender leaves produces long, wiry stems with brightly coloured, lily-like flowers. The corms of some hybrids may rot off during cold, wet winters, but this can be prevented with a layer of mulch. As the plants get larger, they should be divided regularly to maintain their vigour. Grow in a well-drained position, in sun or partial shade. Mid to late summer.

x crocosmiiflora This must be the hardiest of all the crocosmias, and one so often seen that it can be taken for granted. Gently arched stems of vermilion trumpets, heavily washed with orange, are borne in perfect formation above rather invasive mid-green foliage. 60 cm (2 ft).

'Emily McKenzie' This has striking, large, downward-facing flowers of deep orange with a brown dot just inside each petal. 60 cm (2 ft).

'Golden Fleece' Golden-yellow, trumpet-like flowers are carried on gently arching sprays above a clump of light green leaves. 60 cm (2 ft).

'James Coey' A prolific variety with sprays of open, vermilion trumpets with soft orange centres. These are carried on upright, brown stems that arch at the top above rich green leaves. 60 cm (2 ft).

'Lucifer' One of the most handsome varieties with perfect spikes of flaming red, trumpet-shaped flowers. These are produced in profusion and just skim its mid-green, pleated leaves. AGM. 90 cm (3 ft).

'Mars' A short plant with a mass of upright stems that end in gentle sprays of burnt-orange, trumpet-like flowers. Each bloom has a pronounced yellow centre. 60 cm (2 ft).

masoniorum A plant for bigger borders. It produces vermilion trumpets that are perfectly balanced along arching, dark green stems above a large clump of pleated leaves. A tough and reliable variety. AGM. 120 cm (4 ft).

'Severn Sunrise' A ruck of stems spills out from a thick clump of broad, mid-green leaves. This produces sprays of open, glowing fruity-pink, trumpet-shaped flowers. 60 cm (2 ft).

'Solfaterre' Sprays of small, soft yellow flowers are carried above distinctive bronze-tinted leaves. AGM. 60 cm (2 ft).

'Star of the East' A spreading clump of long, broad leaves with sprays of very large, downward-facing, open, soft tangerine flowers. Late to flower. 75 cm (2½ft).

CYNARA *cardunculus* (Cardoon)

A beautifully formed clump of arching, long, deeply toothed, silver-grey leaves is enough in itself. But later, when the flowers arrive, it is even more spectacular. These are carried on tall, stout stems and look like large, purple thistles. The flowers dry well for floral arrangements and it is easy to grow in any well-drained soil in sun. AGM. Summer. 150 cm (5 ft).

CYNOGLOSSUM *nervosum* (Hound's Tongue)

Small, vivid blue flowers are carried in loose sprays on long, arching stems above a clump of hairy leaves. This is a plant for the middle of a border that will provide a misty effect and which mixes well with clump-forming plants, such as hardy geraniums. Plant in any well-drained soil, in sun or partial shade. Mid spring into summer. 60 cm (2 ft).

Crocosmia masoniorum

Crocosmia 'Severn Sunrise'

Crocosmia 'Solfaterre'

Crocosmia 'Star of the East'

Cynara cardunculus

Cynoglossum nervosum

DARMERA *peltata*

An unusual plant that bears its flowers way before the leaves emerge. Flat, broad heads of tiny, pink flowers are carried on upright, sturdy, hairy stems. Some weeks later, shiny, round, mid-green leaves appear. It is useful for the edge of boggy areas or streams where its rhizomous roots will gently spread. Grow in sun or partial shade. AGM. Spring. 90 cm (3 ft).

DELPHINIUM

Once upon a time no self-respecting herbaceous border would be without its collection of these distinguished plants. They produce thick, upright stems that end in long, dense spikes of open blooms. These emerge from a clump of delicately fingered, mid-green leaves. In recent years they have been developed into rigid 'show-bench' specimens. Although they have never been the most labour-saving of perennials, they are still a must for adding height to a border and excellent for flower arrangements. Seed-grown hybrids tend to vary in colour and are generally considered to be of a weaker constitution. However, in my experience if they are given good growing conditions, they will perform almost as well as the more expensive plants that are prepared by vegetative division. To get the best results, they need a good, deeply dug soil with a lot of humus, in sun. In windy areas, they will need staking. Summer.

'**Astolat**' A variety grown from seed with soft lilac-pink flowers. 180 cm (6 ft).

'**Alice Artindale**' Slender spikes of double, blue flowers with highlights of lilac. Each petal curls back to form a decorative button above grey-green leaves. 180 cm (6 ft).

'**Black Knight**' Another plant multiplied by seed with dark blue flowers. 180 cm (6 ft).

'**Butterball**' Very handsome thick spikes of creamy white flowers each with a soft yellow centre. 180 cm (6 ft).

'**Crown Jewels**' Bright, but soft blue flowers, the petals layered to form a semi-double bloom with a large black centre. 120 cm (4 ft).

'**Faust**' Dark blue flowers with black centres, tinted purple at the edges and carried in gently tapering spikes. AGM. 240 cm (8 ft).

Darmera peltata

Delphinium 'Astolat'

Delphinium 'Alice Artindale'

Delphinium 'Butterball'

Delphinium 'Black Knight'

Delphinium 'Faust'

Delphinium 'Crown Jewels'

Delphinium 'Gillian Dallas'

'Gillian Dallas' Perfect spikes of soft powdery lilac-blue flowers with ruffled petals and a white centre. AGM. 150 cm (5 ft).

'Nimrod' Purple flowers with white centres and petals touched with rich blue. 240 cm (8 ft).

'Peracleas' Pale blue flowers with a white centre shaped like a bee. 180 cm (6 ft).

'Summer Skies' Soft blue flowers with a violet tint. A variety grown from seed. 180 cm (6 ft).

'Tiddles' Very soft lilac, double flowers set evenly up sturdy stems. 180 cm (6 ft).

Delphinium 'Summer Skies'

Delphinium 'Peracleas'

Delphinium 'Nimrod'

Delphinium 'Tiddles'

Deschampsia c. 'Bronzeschleier'

Deschampsia c. 'Goldgehange'

Deschampsia c. 'Goldtau'

Dianthus 'Doris'

DESCHAMPSIA *cestpitosa* (Hair Grass)

These are graceful, airy grasses which produce tussocks of fine leaves and upright stems of delicate flowers. They are perfect for planting with large, daisy-shaped perennials and as they freely self-seed, they are liable to travel about the garden. If this is an unwanted quality, dead head them once the flowers have set seed. Grow in soils that do not dry out, in sun or shade. Midsummer.

'Bronzeschleier' A misty plume of silvery flowers turns gentle golden brown with age. 75 cm (2½ft).

'Goldgehange' Golden-yellow flowers. 90 cm (3 ft).

'Goldtau' Green-yellow flowers. Not a vigorous variety. 75 cm (2½ft).

DIANTHUS (Border Pink)

There are literally hundreds of pinks, but I have found only a few to be good border plants. They produce spiky, grey-green foliage, from which appears a continuous succession of rosette-shaped, heavily fragrant flowers. If they need to be tidied up after blooming, make sure they are not trimmed too much, or they will fail to shoot again in spring. Grow in any well-drained soil, in sun. Summer.

'Doris' Rosettes of soft salmon-pink with a deeper centre. This is often sold as a cut flower and has an excellent fragrance. AGM. 15 cm (6 in).

'Houndspool Ruby' Smooth, deep rose-pink flowers. A sport of D. 'Doris'. AGM. 15 cm (6 in).

'Mrs Sinkins' One of the oldest surviving varieties with white, rather ragged, extremely fragrant flowers. 15 cm (6 in).

Dianthus 'Houndspool Ruby'

Dianthus 'Mrs Sinkins'

Dianthus 'Laced Monarch'

Dianthus 'Tamsin'

'Laced Monarch' Large, double flowers of rich pink. These are highlighted with maroon in the centre of each petal. 15 cm (6 in).

'Tamsin' Small, highly fragrant, fringed white petals, edged and marked with pink. AGM. 15 cm (6 in).

DICENTRA (Bleeding Heart)

The unique flowers of this charming group of plants all produce dangling, heart-shaped blooms and mounds of much divided, rather brittle, almost translucent foliage. There are two distinctive types; one is tall and upright, the other produces low, spreading clumps. They are wonderful for spring borders and lightly shaded spots. Grow in a well-drained soil that does not dry out, in sun or partial shade. Spring.

'Bacchanal' Small sprays of slim, rich pink-red flowers are produced in quantity above a low, spreading hummock of mid-green foliage. 45 cm (18 in).

formosa Soft grey-green foliage forms a delicate background to mauve-pink flowers, shaped like slim lockets. 30 cm (1 ft).

formosa alba Low clumps of lush, blue-grey foliage bears arching stems with clusters of slim, pure white flowers. 30 cm (1 ft).

'Langtrees' Slim, white, pink-tinted flowers hang in thick clusters above a creeping carpet of blue-grey foliage. AGM. 45 cm (18 in).

Dicentra 'Bacchanal'

Dicentra 'Langtrees'

Dicentra formosa

Dicentra formosa alba

'Luxuriant' Slender flowers of pink-red are borne above leaves of mid-green. AGM. 60 cm (2 ft).

spectabilis A very handsome, succulent plant with fleshy, soft, maroon-tinted, gently arched stems. These carry a row of fat, heart-shaped, red-pink flowers, each with a long teardrop, above lush, divided rich green foliage. For some reason it is always pictured with tree peonies in Chinese catalogues. AGM. 75 cm (2½ft).

spectabilis **'Alba'** Bright, but soft green foliage bears even paler stems that are beautifully hung with pure white flowers. This is not as tall as its pink sister. AGM. 60 cm (2 ft).

'Stuart Boothman' A creeping clump of red-grey, bronze-tinted, feathery leaves sprouts early and produces small clusters of slim, red-pink flowers. AGM. 30 cm (1 ft).

DICTAMNUS (Dittany, Burning Bush)

A very handsome plant with dense, upright spikes of open flowers, each petal splaying outwards to reveal a few long stamens. It produces a thick clump of lemon-scented, dark green, divided leaves and when the flowers fade, they turn into decorative geometrically shaped pods. Although this is slow to establish, when happy it can be left undivided for years. Grow in any well-drained soil, in sun. Early summer.

albus Purest white flowers with bright green foliage. AGM. 90 cm (3 ft).

albus purpureus Soft mauve flowers painted with deeper coloured veins. AGM. 90 cm (3 ft).

Dicentra 'Luxuriant'

Dicentra 'Stuart Boothman'

Dicentra spectabilis

Dicentra spectabilis 'Alba'

Dictamnus albus

Dictamnus albus purpureus

Dierama pulcherrimum

Digitalis ferruginea

Digitalis grandiflora

DIERAMA *pulcherrimum*
(Angel's Fishing Rod, Wand Flower)

Long stems, like those of a delicate grass, arch most gracefully and carry dangling, conical bells of bright pink. These are borne above a tufted clump of slim foliage. It can be rather tender until established. Plant in a rich, well-drained soil in sun. Midsummer. 120 cm (4 ft).

DIGITALIS (Foxglove)

This most elegant family of perennials could not be easier to grow. Long tubular bells are borne up strong, erect stems above whorls of leaves. Some varieties listed are biennial, but as they continue to self-propagate through liberal seed production, they are worthy of inclusion. All can be happily included in borders or wilder spots in sun or partial shade, but the soil should not be too dry or too wet. They are ideally suited to damp climates, as the flowers never look damaged during periods of extended rain.

ferruginea Honey-coloured flowers, looking rather like choir boys in full song, are carried above rosettes of slender, evergreen, deep green foliage. Early summer. 90 cm (3 ft).

grandiflora (Yellow Foxglove) This gentle plant produces large, soft yellow flowers above mid-green leaves. AGM. Summer. 90 cm (3 ft).

lutea Small, slim bells of soft yellow are massed on short stems above a base of dark green leaves. Late spring into summer. 60 cm (2 ft).

x mertonensis Like *D. grandiflora*, this produces large, softly textured flowers, but these are dusky pink. The leaves are deep green and it comes true from seed. AGM. Late summer to early autumn. 75 cm ($2\frac{1}{2}$ ft).

purpurea albiflora The wild European foxglove of woodlands and dry banks is one of the most beautiful of wild flowers. It produces long graceful stems of large, tubular flowers. In this pure white form it is at its most attractive and under the light shade of trees it will positively glow. As this is a biennial, allow it to self-seed into a natural rhythm. Spring into summer. 150 cm (5 ft).

Digitalis lutea

Digitalis x mertonensis

Digitalis purpurea albiflora

Doronicum x excelsum 'Harpur Crewe'

Echinacea purpurea

purpurea **'Sutton's Apricot'** This is a soft pink variation of *D. purpurea albiflora* and another biennial. Its flowers are heavily brushed with apricot and combine beautifully with blue and soft pink flowers, such as peonies. AGM. Spring into summer. 150 cm (5 ft).

DORONICUM x *excelsum* 'Harpur Crewe' (Leopard's Bane)

A cheerful plant with flat, disc-shaped, finely rayed flowers of bright yellow carried on branched, upright, hairy stems. The leaves are soft green, heart-shaped and toothed around the edges. It forms a slowly spreading clump and is ideal for lightly shaded areas as well as open borders. Grow in a well-drained soil that does not dry out, in sun or partial shade. Spring. 60 cm (2 ft).

ECHINACEA (Coneflower)

These majestic plants are ideal for anyone who likes wildlife in the garden, as they attract both bees and butterflies. They produce large, daisy-shaped flowers, each with relaxed petals and a conelike centre of ginger. The flowers are carried individually on rigid stems with deep green leaves and forms an upright, gently spreading clump. Perfect for a late summer border, they are easy to grow in any well-drained soil, in sun or partial shade. Late summer.

purpurea Deep red-mauve flowers. 105 cm (3½ ft).

purpurea **'White Swan'** Creamy white flowers. 60 cm (2 ft).

Echinacea purpurea 'White Swan'

Digitalis purpurea 'Sutton's Apricot'

Echinops bannaticus 'Taplow Blue'

Echinops 'Nivalis'

Echinops ritro

Echinops ritro 'Veitch's Blue'

Echinops sphaerocephalus 'Arctic Glow'

Epilobium augustifolium album

ECHINOPS (Globe Thistle)

These fit into the bracket of 'architectural' plants and are perfect for the borders of high summer. They produce spiky, sculpted balls of tiny, starry flowers that are borne on tall, stiff stems. Below these is a clump of long, deeply divided leaves. They will grow in a wide range of situations from dry soils in sun (although the leaves may shrivel) to moist spots in semi-shade. The poorer the soil, the better. Summer.

bannaticus **'Taplow Blue'** Pale blue heads of flowers and mid-green foliage. AGM. 120 cm (4 ft).

'Nivalis' A robust plant with soft green leaves and large balls of white flowers. 180 cm (6 ft).

ritro Large, soft steely-blue globes with deep green, spiky leaves that are white beneath. AGM. 120 cm (4 ft).

ritro **'Veitch's Blue'** Small, tightly packed balls of rich deep blue and mid-green leaves. 90 cm (3 ft).

sphaerocephalus **'Arctic Glow'** A recent introduction. This produces ball-like flowers of white that are carried on pale mauve stems with soft grey-green foliage. 90 cm (3 ft).

EPILOBIUM *augustifolium album* (Willow Herb)

In the wild a swathe of pink willow herb is a gentle sight, but in this white form it gains an elegance that benefits large borders or wild areas of the garden. It produces elegant spikes of simple, flat flowers with long stamens and pointed soft green leaves. This is a prolific self-seeder that will grow in any well-drained soil, particularly a poor one, in sun or partial shade. Summer. 150 cm (5 ft).

EPIMEDIUM
(Barrenwort, Bishop's Mitre)

These early flowering plants are not as common in gardens as they should be, which is a shame. Low mounds of heart-shaped leaves, sometimes evergreen, produce small, nodding flowers that are undemonstrative and subtle. Once established, they can happily remain untouched for years, spreading slowly and requiring little attention. They grow in any soil, including a fairly dry one, in partial or full shade. Spring.

x cantabrigiense The flowers of this variety are so subtle they could be missed. These are small, apricot in colour with a yellow centre and borne in sprays on long arching stems. This is a delightful spreading, evergreen plant with fresh green foliage that turns glossy with age. AGM. 30 cm (1 ft).

grandiflorum Lilac flowers with pronounced spurs that spread out like the pointed edges of a professor's hat. These gently nod above a low, spreading clump of leaves that are long and pointed, and bronze coloured when young. 30 cm (1 ft).

grandiflorum **'Lilafee'** A pretty variety with dark violet flowers and white tipped spurs. These dangle like hats above foliage that is purple when young. 23 cm (9 in).

pinnatum colchicum Sprays of primrose-yellow flowers are borne on long, upright stems with evergreen, olive foliage. AGM. 30 cm (1 ft).

Epimedium x cantabrigiense

Epimedium grandiflorum

Epimedium pinnatum colchicum

Epimedium grandiflorum 'Lilafee'

Epimedium pubigerum

Epimedium x rubrum

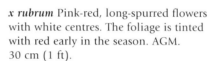

pubigerum A delicate plant with upright stems of very small, white, bell-shaped flowers tinged with red. Evergreen foliage. 45 cm (18 in).

x rubrum Pink-red, long-spurred flowers with white centres. The foliage is tinted with red early in the season. AGM. 30 cm (1 ft).

x versicolor 'Sulphureum' A robust plant with yellow centred, cream flowers that flutter just above a dense mound of evergreen leaves. In winter these are burnished with brown. AGM. 45 cm (18 in).

x warleyense 'Orangekönigin' This produces soft orange flowers with yellow centres, in open sprays above evergreen leaves. These are heavily tinged with red in winter. 45 cm (18 in).

x youngianum 'Niveum' A delightful plant with mid-green leaves and delicate, small, white, cupped flowers carried on reddish stems. AGM. 30 cm (1 ft).

Epimedium x versicolor 'Sulphureum'

Epimedium x warleyense 'Orangekönigin'

Epimedium x youngianum 'Niveum'

Erigeron 'Dunkelste Aller'

Erigeron 'Rosa Juwel'

Erigeron 'Foersters Liebling'

Erigeron karvinskianus

ERIGERON (Fleabane)

These delightfully conventional plants will sit safely amongst other perennials at the front of a border. A low, spreading clump of mid-green leaves is topped for weeks with sprays of finely rayed, daisy-shaped flowers. They are easy to grow in any well-drained soil that does not dry out, in sun or partial shade. But beware, rabbits love them! Early to midsummer.

'Dunkelste Aller' Deep violet flowers with yellow centres. AGM. 60 cm (2 ft).

'Foersters Liebling' Pink flowers, a little on the lilac side, with large yellow centres. AGM. 60 cm (2 ft).

karvinskianus A prostrate plant with very small leaves. These are smothered for months with a sea of little white and pink daisies. It is an ideal plant for growing in small borders or amongst paving. AGM. 15 cm (6 in).

'Rosa Juwel' Sprays of baby-pink flowers carried on upright stems. 45 cm (18 in).

'Schneewittchen' White daisies, pink beneath, emerge from pink buds. 45 cm (18 in).

ERIOPHYLLUM *lanatum*
(Woolly Sunflower)

A low-growing perennial for the front of the border. Silver, chrysanthemum-shaped leaves form a spreading clump that is smothered for weeks with small golden yellow daisies. It is ideal for a poor soil with good drainage, in sun. Midsummer. 30 cm (1 ft).

Erigeron 'Schneewittchen'

Eriophyllum lanatum

Erodium manescaui

Eryngium agavifolium

Eryngium alpinum

ERODIUM *manescaui* (Heron's Bill)

A bigger member of the 'alpine' family, it produces ample quantities of both flowers and leaves and is suitable for the border. The flowers resemble bright pink hardy geraniums and are borne for weeks on end in starry sprays on stiff stems. These emerge from a central crown of mid-green, deeply toothed leaves. Grow in any well-drained soil, the drier the better, in sun. Summer. 45 cm (18 in).

ERYNGIUM (Sea Holly)

All eryngiums are spiky and here lies their charm. These distinctly abstract plants produce sprays of small flowers. Each bloom forms part of a cone and is seated on a spiny collar of bracts. These are carried on branched, upright stems and emerge from a flat rosette of leaves. The flowers in their dried form, on and off the plant, will look good throughout the winter. They are ideal subjects for coastal gardens, but will grow in any well-drained soil, in sun. Summer.

agavifolium One of the few green varieties. Large, flat whorls of strappy, mid-green leaves with sharks' teeth edging, give rise to strong, upright stems. These bear a candelabra of small, oval, moss-green flowers. Rather exotic and evergreen. 120 cm (4 ft).

alpinum A laced and netted, broad collar of grey-blue creates a beautiful background to a central dome of soft blue. Below, the leaves are deeply divided and mid-green. AGM. 60 cm (2 ft).

giganteum (Miss Willmott's Ghost) Once established, this beautiful biennial gets everywhere, but like many plants that are easy to grow, neglect is the answer to its success. A base of soft green leaves sends up stiff stems with high cones of silver-blue flowers. These are each surrounded by a large silver-grey collar. It freely self-seeds. AGM. 90 cm (3 ft).

horridum A pale green variety with well-branched stems bearing open sprays of small flowers. This is an unfortunate name for an attractive plant. 90 cm (3 ft).

x oliverianum A highly ornamental plant with soft steely blue flowers. These form a large central cone that is surrounded by a broad collar of misty blue, tinged purple towards the centre. AGM. 90 cm (3 ft).

Eryngium giganteum

Eryngium horridum

Eryngium x oliverianum

planum An excellent upright variety for flower arrangements as well as borders. Small, mid-blue flowers, the size of thimbles, are surrounded by a small collar of slim bracts. These are borne on long, very branched, blue stems above mid-green leaves. 90 cm (3 ft).

planum **'Seven Seas'** This carries its thimble-sized cones of soft green on a dense framework of much branched stems. These arise from a rosette of spoonlike, dark green leaves and later, as the flowers emerge, the cones turn to navy blue. 45 cm (18 in).

x tripartitum An impressive mass of small, blue flowers is borne above dark green foliage. Each flower is seated above a spiky collar of slim bracts. AGM. 60 cm (2 ft).

variifolium The glory of this plant lies in its attractive, ground-hugging leaves. These are deep green and marbled with white vein. Later, widely branched stems produce small, silver-blue flowers, each with collars of slim, silver bracts. 45 cm (18 in).

x zabelli A very attractive plant with small, grass-green flowers that become grey-blue with age. These are surrounded by slender, very spiky, silver collars and form a broad clump with well-divided, deep green leaves. 90 cm (3 ft).

ERYSIMUM (Perennial Wallflower)

These are showy, but not brash, perennial wallflowers that, like their annual counterparts, bloom throughout the summer. They form dense mounds with small, mid-green leaves that are covered with clusters of simple, four-petalled flowers. After the blooms have faded dead head them to encourage more flowers. They are rather short-lived plants that should be grown in a fairly poor, very well-drained soil, in sun. Summer.

'Bowles Mauve' Clusters of gentle blue-purple flowers make a fine contrast against its grey-green foliage. This is perfect for growing with silver and blue plants. AGM. 60 cm (2 ft).

'Chelsea Jacket' A prostrate plant for the front of a border, with clusters of flowers that open tangerine and pass to dark pink. AGM. 30 cm (1 ft).

Eryngium planum 'Seven Seas'

Eryngium x tripartitum

Eryngium x zabelli

Eryngium planum

Eryngium variifolium

Erysimum 'Bowles Mauve'

Erysimum 'Chelsea Jacket'

Eupatorium purpureum

Euphorbia amygdaloides 'Purpurea'

EUPATORIUM *purpureum* (Joe-Pye Weed)

An American native with large, fluffy, gently domed, slightly scented heads of tiny, dusky pink flowers. These are carried on top of very upright, purple tinged stems with rough, dark green leaves. Its rather unflattering common name does not do it justice, as it is a grand plant, especially for the back of a border. Grow in any moisture-retentive soil, in sun or partial shade. Midsummer. 150 cm (5 ft).

EUPHORBIA (Spurge, Milkweed)

I would not be without at least one *Euphorbia* in my garden. Tiny flowers are surrounded by large bracts and form an intricate part of the whole plant. These are carried in clusters or spikes on leafy stems. Some varieties form round clumps, while others are low and mounding. Grow in a well-drained soil, in partial shade or sun. Spring.

amygdaloides **'Purpurea'** A compact, round clump of long, viridian-green foliage bears broad spikes of lime-green flowers with long red bracts. This is a handsome plant and combines well with the golden grass *Milium effusum* 'Aureum'. 60 cm (2 ft).

amygdaloides robbiae Small, yellow-green flowers are produced in open sprays above whorls of dark green foliage. It is happy in deep shade and will spread like wildfire once established. AGM. 45 cm (18 in).

characias wulfenii One of my desert island plants. It produces a handsome upright clump with soft, evergreen, grey-green leaves. In midwinter the long stems turn demurely down to protect a cluster of flower buds that open in spring into broad heads of small, lime-green flowers. Grow in flower borders, among shrubs or as a specimen plant. AGM. 120 cm (4 ft).

Euphorbia amygdaloides robbiae

Euphorbia characias wulfenii

Euphorbia cyparissias

Euphorbia cyparissias 'Fens Ruby'

Euphorbia dulcis 'Chameleon'

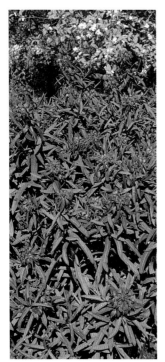

Euphorbia griffithii 'Dixter'

Euphorbia griffithii 'Fireglow'

Euphorbia x martinii

Euphorbia myrsinites

cyparissias Beware of this one unless you want vigorous ground cover. A rapidly spreading sea of short stems, with soft mid-green leaves, is topped with small clusters of vivid lime-green flowers. 15 cm (6 in).

cyparissias **'Fens Ruby'** This grows like *E. cyparissias* but produces rich rust-coloured foliage. 15 cm (6 in).

dulcis **'Chameleon'** An airy mound of rich mahogany-red leaves is highlighted by small lime-green flowers in spring. At first these add just a touch of colour, but as they age, the flowers turn, like the leaves, to brown. This gentle plant can be slow to establish. 30 cm (1 ft).

griffithii **'Dixter'** A beautiful, quietly spreading plant. Erect red stems carry copper-tinted, deep green leaves and are topped with small, orange flowers. The flowers are held in broad heads and are surrounded by large bracts of a distinctive dusky orange. AGM. 90 cm (3 ft).

griffithii **'Fireglow'** Very similar to *E. griffithii* 'Dixter', but with much redder bracts. The foliage later becomes richly tinted with autumn colours. 90 cm (3 ft).

x martinii Upright sprays of light green flowers are carried for weeks above a neat, round clump of foliage. The leaves are of deepest green and tinted underneath with red. AGM. 60 cm (2 ft).

myrsinites A strange sort of dinosaur-like plant. It produces fleshy, blue-grey leaves, like scales, along wandering prostrate stems that end in umbels of lime-green flowers. A useful plant for the front of the border and difficult dry areas. AGM. 15 cm (6 in).

Euphorbia palustris

Euphorbia polychroma

palustris A spectacular, erect plant. An upright clump of tall stems carries lots of light green leaves. In mid spring, these are topped with large, flat heads of sulphur-yellow flowers and in autumn the whole plant turns red. AGM. 90 cm (3 ft).

polychroma A perfectly domed plant with light green leaves and broad heads of bright sulphur-green flowers. AGM. 60 cm (2 ft).

FERULA communis (Giant Fennel)

Large, very finely divided, almost filigree leaves form a mound, from which erupts a thick, grey-green stem. This is branched towards the top and produces domed clusters of small, sulphur-yellow flowers. A true giant, growing to 12 ft or more, for the very back of a border or wilder area. Any well-drained soil, in sun. Summer. 360 cm (12 ft).

FESTUCA *glauca* (Fescue)

A small, clump-forming grass with fine threadlike, blue-grey leaves and tight, fluffy heads of silver flowers. These are produced on upright, ochre stems and turn to buff yellow with time. It is a good plant for bedding out and will grow in most well-drained soils, in sun. Midsummer. 30 cm (1 ft).

Ferula communis

Festuca glauca

FILIPENDULA
(Meadowsweet, Queen-in-the-Meadow)

These are gentle plants. Small, deliciously scented flowers form heads as soft and fluffy as a mohair jumper. Each bloom, with long stamens, opens from a round, dewdrop-like bud and is borne on wiry stems above a clump of vine-shaped leaves. All varieties, except the *F. vulgaris* types, require a well-drained soil that does not dry out, in sun or partial shade. The *F. vulgaris* hybrids are naturally found in wet or very damp areas, such as ditches along roads, and prefer a soil that remains moist or wet throughout the summer. Midsummer.

palmata '**Rosea**' Round mounds of large leaves and bronze-red stems carry small flowers of bright pink that quickly fade to white. Sweetly scented. 120 cm (4 ft).

purpurea Vibrant pink-purple flowers are carried in wispy sprays above deep green foliage. AGM. 120 cm (4 ft).

purpurea albiflora This produces clean white flowers and dark green leaves. 120 cm (4 ft).

ulmaria '**Aurea**' A dramatic yellow-leaved plant, especially when young, that later turns lime-green. It has white flowers, which makes it a good plant for brightening up a dull, damp spot. 45 cm (18 in).

vulgaris '**Multiplex**' Broad, flat heads of double, creamy-white flowers are carried above dark green leaves. 60 cm (2 ft).

FOENICULUM *vulgare* '**Purpureum**'
(Bronze Fennel)

A handsome culinary herb, invaluable for adding soft colour and form to a herbaceous border. Large plumes of reddish-grey foliage, fluffy as a boa feather, produce tall stems that end in umbels of small, mustard-yellow flowers. Unless you want a Triffid-like invasion, remove the seeds before they disperse. The whole plant is aniseed-scented and naturally found at coastal edges. It thrives in any well-drained soil, in sun. Midsummer to autumn. 180 cm (6 ft).

Filipendula purpurea

Filipendula palmata 'Rosea'

Filipendula purpurea albiflora

Filipendula ulmaria 'Aurea'

Filipendula vulgaris 'Multiplex'

Foeniculum vulgare 'Purpureum'

Fragaria 'Red Ruby'

Fragaria 'Pink Panda'

FRAGARIA (Strawberry)

From one tall culinary plant to a very small one. An evergreen base of large, toothed leaves is dotted for weeks with simple, yellow-centred flowers. They make excellent, if vigorous, ground-cover plants that propel themselves around by sending out runners. These can easily be hoisted out if unwanted. I allow these plants to meander amongst shrubby plants and herbs, such as rosemary. Plant in well-drained soil, in sun or partial shade. Late spring into autumn.

'Pink Panda' The flowers are a rather startling colour. Lipstick-pink, neither bright nor gentle, with deep green leaves. 15 cm (6 in).

'Red Ruby' Vibrant pink-red flowers, a colour you either love or hate. It mixes well with low-growing soft pink or lilac flowers, such as *Veronica* 'Ellen Mae'. 15 cm (6 in).

vesca **'Variegata'** Simple white flowers are set against a background of white splashed, mid-green foliage. It sometimes produces small fruits. Pull out the non-variegated foliage before it takes over. 15 cm (6 in).

FRANCOA *ramosa* (Bridal Wreath)

Slender, upright stems finish in open spikes of small, white flowers, each striped with pink. These are borne above a tight rosette of oval, mid-green leaves. It makes a good pot plant and is ideal for paved areas or small borders. Grow in a well-drained soil, in sun or partial shade. Summer. 45 cm (18 in).

Fragaria vesca 'Variegata'

Francoa ramosa

Gaillardia 'Burgunder'

Gaillardia 'Dazzler'

Gaillardia 'Tokajer'

Galega officinalis

GAILLARDIA (Blanket Flower)

A rather short-lived, but joyful perennial from North America. It produces a long succession of large, daisy-shaped flowers on slender stems amid long, mid-green leaves. These form low clumps which can look rather untidy, but they are easy to grow in a very well-drained soil in sun. Summer.

'Burgunder' Rich brown-red flowers with a centre of the same colour. 60 cm (2 ft).

'Dazzler' A summery flower with deep mahogany-red, yellow tipped petals. AGM. 60 cm (2 ft).

'Tokajer' Bright orange flowers with a flush of maroon at the base of each petal. 75 cm (2½ft).

GALEGA (Goat's Rue)

This wild plant of Europe and Asia produces a large, leafy bush of mid-green leaves. These are borne in ladder formation and are decorated with short spikes of pea-like flowers. They are robust plants, ideal for big borders or wild areas. Grow in any very well-drained soil, including poor ones, in sun. Midsummer.

officinalis Soft lilac flowers with white lower petals. 120 cm (4 ft).

officinalis **'Alba'** Pure white flowers. 120 cm (4 ft).

orientalis Rich lilac-blue flowers borne in slim spikes with pale green leaves. This is a perfect plant for growing with pink old roses. 120 cm (4 ft).

Galega officinalis 'Alba'

Galega orientalis

Galium odoratum

GALIUM *odoratum* (Sweet Woodruff)

A lush plant that produces a thick, ground -overing carpet. Its bright green leaves are narrow, pointed, rough to the touch and borne in whorls. In spring, these are covered with clusters of small, starry, white, faintly scented flowers. A plant that can be invasive, it is useful for shady spots. Grow in any well-drained soil, in sun or partial shade. Spring. 30 cm (1 ft).

GAURA

These are wonderful for planting schemes that need airy and graceful plants. Slender stems with oval, mid-green leaves produce lots of delicate open flowers, each with elegant, long stamens. It is a rather short-lived perennial that will thrive in any well-drained soil, in sun. Summer.

lindheimeri Pure white flowers. AGM. 90 cm (3 ft).

lindheimeri **'Siskiyou Pink'** White flowers, each heavily flushed with deep pink. 75 cm (2½ft).

GENTIANA (Gentian)

There are only a few gentians large enough to be included as border plants. These are a little fussy about their growing conditions, needing a moist, humus-rich soil in partial shade, but once established they will survive untouched for years. Late summer.

asclepiadea (Willow Gentian) This tumbling plant produces a mass of long stems with pointed, dark green leaves each housing a cluster of dark indigo-blue trumpets. It increases slowly and is ideal for planting along shady, woodland streams. AGM. 90 cm (3 ft).

lutea (Bitterwort, Yellow Gentian) Bell-shaped, straw-yellow flowers are carried in candelabra-style whorls on upright stems above broad, mid-green leaves. 150 cm (5 ft).

tibetica A curious plant that grows near to the ground. It produces a cluster of large, yellowish flowers that nestle into the centre of a rosette of large, pointed, deep green leaves. 30 cm (1 ft).

Gaura lindheimeri 'Siskiyou Pink'

Gentiana asclepiadea

Gaura lindheimeri

Gentiana lutea

Gentiana tibetica

GERANIUM
(Cranesbill, Hardy Geranium)

I make no excuses for including so many Hardy Geraniums. They not only provide constant colour throughout summer with a long succession of small flowers, they are also tough and versatile. Their foliage, borne in dense mounds, adds a soft tapestry to a border of any style. Indeed, they are some of the easiest perennials to accommodate around the garden. In traditional borders, grow them with delphiniums, lupins and roses. In larger planting schemes, the more robust varieties can be mixed with daisy-flowered plants and grasses. The smaller types are excellent for planting along edges, amongst paving or in small borders. They are all easy to grow, but some varieties, particularly the larger ones, may need a little controlling. These will require frequent division and if the whole plant is cut back after blooming, more flowers and tidier growth will be produced. Grow in any soil that does not dry out, but is not waterlogged, in partial shade or sun.

'Ann Folkard' An open, trailing plant with long stems that terminate in flat, purple-violet flowers with black centres surrounded by black eyelashes. The leaves, when young, are yellow and later pass to soft green. I allow it to scramble through and amongst other herbaceous plants. AGM. Midsummer into autumn. 45 cm (18 in).

x cantabrigiense A small variety useful for border edges and between paving. It produces a carpet of shiny, round leaves that is smothered with flat, lilac-pink flowers. Late spring into summer. 23 cm (9 in).

x cantabrigiense **'Biokovo'** Like G. *x cantabrigiense*, but with pure white flowers. Late spring into summer. 23 cm (9 in).

cinereum **'Laurence Flatman'** A low, mounding plant with cupped, soft pink flowers. These have dark centres, veined with maroon and are carried above small, round, mid-green leaves. Midsummer. 23 cm (9 in).

clarkei **'Kashmir Pink'** Open flowers of soft pink, one of the most pink of all geraniums. Early summer. 45 cm (18 in).

clarkei **'Kashmir White'** An excellent border variety with pure white, cupped flowers, delicately veined with lilac. These are borne just above a round clump of deeply divided foliage. AGM. Early summer. 45 cm (18 in).

Geranium 'Ann Folkard'

Geranium x cantabrigiense

Geranium x cantabrigiense 'Biokovo'

Geranium cinereum 'Laurence Flatman'

Geranium clarkei 'Kashmir White'

Geranium clarkei 'Kashmir Pink'

Geranium endressii

Geranium himalayense 'Gravetye'

endressii A rampant little number smattered with a constant succession of large, bright blue-pink, funnel-shaped flowers. These are sprinkled above a semi-evergreen mound of light green leaves. AGM. Summer. 45 cm (18 in).

fremontii An upright plant that is a little different, or should I say a different variation, from many other types. Strong, hairy stems and large, soft, mid-green leaves are topped with nodding clusters of flat, violet flowers. It is useful for less formal borders or wild areas. Early summer. 60 cm (2 ft).

himalayense **'Gravetye'** A border plant with very divided, mid-green, almost frilly leaves that form round clumps. These are dotted with open, mid-blue flowers, the centres of which are white and distinctively veined with purple. AGM. Late spring to late summer. 45 cm (18 in).

'Johnson's Blue' Probably the best-known blue border variety. Open, saucer-shaped flowers of bright blue are produced in profusion above a tidy mound of divided, dark green leaves. AGM. Late spring into summer. 60 cm (2 ft).

macrorrhizum A plant for shady places with round, deeply cut, scented, rich green leaves. It forms a thick, spreading carpet, covered with small, flat, rich pink flowers that pop from red calyces. The whole plant, leaves and flowers, has a reddish-pink quality and is smaller than the named forms. Spring. 30 cm (1 ft).

macrorrhizum **'Album'** Pure white flowers with long pink stamens. AGM. Spring. 45 cm (18 in).

Geranium fremontii

Geranium 'Johnson's Blue'

Geranium macrorrhizum

Geranium macrorrhizum 'Album'

Geranium macrorrhizum 'Ingwersen's Variety'

macrorrhizum 'Ingwersen's Variety'
I think that this is the prettiest variety of
G. *macrorrhizum,* with soft pink flowers.
AGM. Spring. 45 cm (18 in).

x magnificum Clusters of deep blue,
cupped flowers are borne just above a
tight clump of rounded leaves. In autumn
these turn red for a short time. I consider
this to be the best deep blue hardy
geranium for mixing amongst other
perennials in a border. AGM. Late spring
to early summer. 75 cm (2½ ft).

nodosum An excellent plant for shady
places. It produces a continuous
smattering of little, lilac-pink trumpets
over a dense hummock of pointed, glossy
leaves. Late spring to autumn.
30 cm (1 ft).

x oxonianum hybrids

These were originally crosses between G.
endressii and G. *versicolor,* consequently all
the flowers are pink and trumpet-shaped.
They are perfect for planting in cottage-
style gardens and traditional herbaceous
borders, as they bloom more continuously
than all other pink geraniums. The foliage
forms dense weed-excluding mounds, but
beware, they are pernicious in their seed
production and can turn a border into a
sea of pink. Culling may be essential.
Early to late summer.

x oxonianum 'A.T. Johnson' Shallow
trumpets of silver-pink, finely veined with
magenta, flower almost continuously
throughout the summer. AGM.
60 cm (2 ft).

x oxonianum 'Claridge Druce' Large,
open trumpets of bright pink, veined with
magenta are held above a mound of mid-
green leaves. It produces a good second
crop of flowers. 45 cm (18 in).

Geranium x magnificum

Geranium nodosum

Geranium x oxonianum 'Claridge Druce'

Geranium x oxonianum 'A.T. Johnson'

Geranium x oxonianum 'Patricia Josephine'

Geranium x oxonianum thurstonianum

Geranium x oxonianum 'Wargrave Pink'

Geranium x oxonianum 'Widecombe'

Geranium phaeum

x oxonianum **'Patricia Josephine'** I am unashamedly including one of my own finds. A robust clump of mid-green leaves is covered throughout the summer with very pale pink flowers. These fade to almost white with age. This seedling turned up in my mother's garden, which is, to say the least, ecological in its self-seeding nature. 75 cm (2½ ft).

x oxonianum **thurstonianum** A plant generous in its quantity of flower. These are little, deep pink and veined with cerise. Sometimes they produce a further inner ring of petals to make them double. 60 cm (2 ft).

x oxonianum **'Wargrave Pink'** Clear salmon-pink, funnel-like flowers – a rather yellow pink that can be difficult to mix with other colours. These are carried above a tidy mound of small, soft green foliage. AGM. 60 cm (2 ft).

x oxonianum **'Widecombe'** A neat, tight, hummock of leaves is covered with bright pink, trumpet-shaped flowers. These fade to white as they age to give the whole plant a two-tone feel. It is not a vigorous variety. 45 cm (18 in).

phaeum (Mourning Widow) A wonderful common name for a flower that mimics a bonneted lady with her head tilted sadly forward. Clusters of glossy, black-purple flowers are pinched back to reveal white stamens. These are carried on erect stems, well above a mound of round leaves. All the G. *phaeum* varieties are excellent for providing early flowers in shady places. Spring. 90 cm (3 ft).

phaeum **'Album'** Sprays of clearest white flowers. Spring. 90 cm (3 ft).

phaeum **'Lily Lovell'** Pure purple flowers. Spring. 90 cm (3 ft).

phaeum lividum Soft rosy-lilac flowers, a colour that is hard to describe. Spring. 90 cm (3 ft).

Geranium phaeum 'Album'

Geranium phaeum 'Lily Lovell'

Geranium phaeum lividum

phaeum 'Samobor' Dark purple flowers are borne above a clump of mid-green leaves, each marked with a large purple circle in the centre. Spring. 90 cm (3 ft).

Phillippe Vapelle This must be a hybrid of *G. renardii*. It produces open, soft lilac flowers that are borne in clusters above a mound of velvety, round, mid-green foliage. 30 cm (1 ft).

pratense **albiflorum** (Meadow Cranesbill) The wild blue form, *G. pratense*, can be found along lanes of southern England as well as throughout Europe, but this is a far prettier form. It produces saucer-like, white flowers that, if grown from seed, will vary in colour tone. Late spring into summer. 90 cm (3 ft).

pratense '**Mrs. Kendal Clark**' A handsome variety. This produces flat, grey-blue flowers, marbled with white veins, which are held above divided, mid-green leaves. These become tinted with red in autumn. AGM. Late spring into summer. 90 cm (3 ft).

pratense '**Plenum Caeruleum**' A plant with small double, slate-blue flowers that look like neat rosettes. They are borne in sprays just above divided, fernlike, soft green leaves. Summer. 90 cm (3 ft).

pratense '**Striatum**' A most charming variety with cupped, blue flowers that are heavily striped and spotted with white. Although it is variable from seed, most seedlings will come true to type. Late spring into summer. 90 cm (3 ft).

Geranium Phillippe Vapelle

Geranium pratense 'Mrs. Kendal Clark'

Geranium pratense 'Plenum Caeruleum'

Geranium phaeum 'Samobor'

Geranium pratense albiflorum

Geranium pratense 'Striatum'

Geranium psilostemon

Geranium renardii

psilostemon The tallest variety with intense cerise-pink, black-eyed flowers carried over a clump of refined foliage. This needs to be grown with space around it, perhaps towards the back of a border. AGM. Summer. 120 cm (4 ft).

psilostemon 'Bressingham Flair' Large, open flowers of purple-pink, each with a black eye, are held just above deeply cut, mid-green leaves. This is a more useful plant than G. *psilostemon*, as it suits all sizes of garden. Summer. 60 cm (2 ft).

renardii A distinctive little border plant with round, soft green leaves with a texture similar to that of culinary Sage. These form a neat dome that, for a brief period, is covered with clusters of lilac veined, white, saucer-like flowers. AGM. Spring. 45 cm (18 in).

x riversleaianum 'Mavis Simpson' While the next variety has the 'AGM', I think this is a better plant. It produces small, silvery-pink, saucer-shaped blooms above a spreading mound of neatly divided, soft green, silver-edged leaves. It is very continuous in its flowering and an ideal edging plant. All summer. 15 cm (6 in).

x riversleaianum 'Russell Prichard' Flat, rich pink flowers are scattered in profusion over a carpet of deep green leaves. I find this is liable to die in cold, wet winters. AGM. Summer. 23 cm (9 in).

sanguineum A low-growing variety with flat, rose-purple flowers, veined with magenta. These are carried above a spreading mound of deeply divided, dark green leaves. Early summer. 23 cm (9 in).

Geranium psilostemon 'Bressingham Flair'

Geranium x riversleaianum 'Russell Prichard'

Geranium x riversleaianum 'Mavis Simpson'

Geranium sanguineum

Geranium sanguineum 'Album'

Geranium sanguineum 'Glenluce'

Geranium sanguineum 'Max Frei'

Geranium sanguineum striatum

sanguineum 'Album' Large, saucer-shaped flowers of purest white, skim a thick mat of deeply cut, mid-green foliage. Ideal for the front of a border. AGM. Summer. 23 cm (9 in).

sanguineum 'Glenluce' A sea of glossy, deep green leaves, small and round, is studded with lavender-pink, cupped flowers. This is the tallest of the G. *sanguineum* varieties. Late spring. 30 cm (1 ft).

sanguineum 'Max Frei' Large, cupped flowers of vivid magenta with foliage that is richly tinted red-bronze in autumn. Summer. 23 cm (9 in).

Geranium sylvaticum 'Album'

sanguineum striatum One of the prettiest of the low-growing varieties, with flat mounds of leaves and sprays of pale pink flowers. AGM. Summer. 23 cm (9 in).

sylvaticum 'Album' An erect plant with sprays of white flowers carried in bunches on upright stems above a basal clump of fingered, light green leaves. AGM. Late spring. 75 cm (2½ft).

sylvaticum 'Amy Doncaster' A mass of rich blue flowers, each with a white eye. These are held in clusters on upright stems, which just about obliterate the dense clump of soft green foliage. Late spring into summer. 75 cm (2½ft).

sylvaticum 'Mayflower' A plant with marvellously rich violet-blue flowers. Like all G. *sylvaticum* varieties, it is upright in habit and indispensable for early colour. Late spring. 75 cm (2½ft).

versicolor A low, spreading plant for lightly shaded areas. It produces white flowers that are distinctively drawn with red veins. With age these veins pass to a shiny, deep pink. Summer. 30 cm (1 ft).

Geranium sylvaticum 'Amy Doncaster'

Geranium versicolor

Geranium sylvaticum 'Mayflower'

Geranium wallichianum 'Buxton's Blue'

Geranium wlassovianum

Geum coccineum

Geum 'Dolly North'

wallichianum 'Buxton's Blue' A prostrate plant with red-tinted leaves and bright blue, disc-shaped flowers, each with a large, white eye. It is slow to establish and needs a very well-drained soil. AGM. Midsummer into autumn. 15 cm (6 in).

wlassovianum The last *Geranium* to flower. Sprays of small, intensely purple flowers lie above a spreading clump of round, gently divided, soft mid-green leaves. These are brushed around the edges with maroon and turn rich red in autumn. Late summer to autumn. 60 cm (2 ft).

GEUM (Avens)

The wild form of these pretty plants can be found in damp areas throughout Europe. The flowers are borne in loose sprays on slender stems above a dense mound of broad, hairy, mid-green leaves. The cultivated varieties are extremely hardy and ideal for planting at the front of a border. They need a sunny position with soil that does not dry out during summer.

coccineum Single, orange-red, cupped flowers with prominent golden stamens. Late spring. 45 cm (18 in).

'Dolly North' Double flowers of bright orange that look like prize rosettes. Early summer. 45 cm (18 in).

'Georgenberg' Rich orange-yellow, single flowers. Late spring. 30 cm (1 ft).

'Lady Stratheden' A free-flowering variety with double, glowing yellow blooms carried on upright stems. This is excellent for adding a splash of colour to the front of a border. AGM. Late spring into summer. 45 cm (18 in).

'Mrs. J. Bradshaw' A robust plant with ruffled, semi-double, scarlet flowers and yellow centres. AGM. Late spring into summer. 45 cm (18 in).

rivale (Water Avens) A European native with nodding, bell-like flowers in colours that range from dusky pink to deep orange-red. Spring. 30 cm (1 ft).

Geum 'Georgenberg'

Geum 'Lady Stratheden'

Geum 'Mrs. J. Bradshaw'

Geum rivale

GILLENIA *trifoliata*
(Bowman's Root, Indian Physic)

This is a delightful plant. It produces loose sprays of small, starry, pure white flowers, each seated in red calyces. These are carried on red stems that form a dense, upright clump with oval, pointed, mid-green leaves. In autumn, they continue to be attractive as the leaves turn to bright red and orange. Plant in a well-drained soil, in sun or partial shade. AGM. Midsummer. 90 cm (3 ft).

GUNNERA *manicata*

This monster of a plant is distinctly sinister. It produces immense round, divided leaves, like great parasols, on thick stems that are smattered with roselike thorns. From its interior a large, conelike flower of mid-green appears. This is a truly unusual plant for wet conditions and a must for larger ponds or streams, where it can remain undisturbed for years. It may need some protection from severe frosts during winter. AGM. Summer. 240 cm (8 ft).

GYPSOPHILA

Frothy sprays of tiny, round flowers are carried on a network of slim stems with a light amount of foliage at the base. It is a useful border plant for hiding varieties that bloom during spring and then fade in summer to leave a gap. Grow in any well-drained soil in sun. Midsummer.

paniculata **'Bristol Fairy'** (Baby's Breath) Long stems produce broad sprays of small, pure white, pompon-like flowers. This is a flower arranger's dream as it lasts for weeks as a cut bloom. Florists often refer to it as 'Gyp'. AGM. 90 cm (3 ft).

'Rosenschleier' A low-growing plant with tiny, semi-double, white flowers tinged with pink. It forms a spreading mound that is useful for small, dry borders. AGM. 30 cm (1 ft).

Gillenia trifoliata

Gunnera manicata

Gypsophila paniculata 'Bristol Fairy'

Gypsophila 'Rosenschleier'

Helenium 'Chipperfield Orange'

Helenium 'Moerheim Beauty'

Helenium 'The Bishop'

HELENIUM
(Sneezeweed, Helen's Flower)

These are valuable plants for bringing late colour into a mixed border. They produce upright clumps of branched stems lightly clothed with long, mid-green leaves and a mass of daisy-shaped flowers. Each bloom has a prominently domed centre of brown. Grow in a rich, well-drained soil that does not dry out, in sun or partial shade. Late summer into autumn.

'Chipperfield Orange' This produces yellow flowers that are heavily brushed with red. 90 cm (3 ft).

'Moerheim Beauty' A variety with rich red-brown blooms that eventually fade to burnt orange. 90 cm (3 ft).

'The Bishop' A bright plant with rich yellow flowers. The petals are ruffled with pleats and, as the pollen matures, the dark brown centre gradually turns to yellow. 90 cm (3 ft).

'Waldtraut' When young the flowers of this multicoloured variety are golden yellow. As they age, they turn to brick orange with yellow flares, and eventually to red. 60 cm (2 ft).

'Wyndley' A variety with yellow flowers that transform to brick-red with age. 90 cm (3 ft).

Helenium 'Wyndley'

Helenium 'Waldtraut'

Helianthus atrorubens

Helianthus 'Capenoch Star'

Helianthus 'Lemon Queen'

Helianthus 'Monarch'

Helianthus 'Loddon Gold'

HELIANTHUS (Perennial Sunflower)

These cheerful plants are rather coarse, but ideal for the back of a border. The blooms are carried on tall, upright, leafy stems that grow into broad clumps. They can be invasive and frequent division may be needed, not only keep them under control, but to maintain their vigour. Grow in a fertile, well-drained soil that remains moist, in sun. Late summer into early autumn.

atrorubens A golden yellow, semi-double flower with pleated petals and a dark brown centre. The leaves are hairy and mid-green. 150 cm (5 ft).

'Capenoch Star' Bright yellow, daisy-like flowers with a pompon-like centre of short petals and large, heart-shaped leaves. It makes a good cut flower. AGM. Late summer into early autumn. 150 cm (5 ft).

'Lemon Queen' A delicate, yet large plant with single, starry, lemon flowers borne above and amongst ample light green leaves. Late summer into early autumn. 210 cm (7 ft).

'Loddon Gold' Double, bright yellow flowers that resemble a large and cheerful dahlia. AGM. Late summer to mid autumn. 150 cm (5 ft).

'Monarch' A shaggy flower of bright yellow is carried on slender, branched stems. Each flower has petals that are pinched at the ends and a brown centre that becomes yellow with pollen. AGM. 180 cm (6 ft).

HELIOPSIS *scabra* 'Incomparabilis' (Ox Eye)

Another one of those yellow, summery, daisy-like plants. However, unlike many of the others, this is suitable for the centre of a wide border. It has double flowers of bright yellow that are borne singly above a wide clump of mid-green leaves. Plant in any well-drained soil, in sun. Late summer. 90 cm (3 ft).

Heliopsis scabra 'Incomparabilis'

Helleborus argutifolius

Helleborus niger

HELLEBORUS (Hellebore)

A very masculine group of plants that would be hard to exclude from any garden. As the winter days lengthen into spring, they begin to bloom, sitting proudly with the flowers of primulas and snowdrops. They bear beautiful, highly ornamental, cupped flowers that are poised elegantly above evergreen leaves. All hellebores are ideal for planting beneath deciduous shrubs and trees, as well as in more shady borders. They prefer a humus-rich, moist soil, in partial shade. Late winter to early spring.

arguifolius A variety that produces thick clusters of round buds that open into shallowly cupped, soft lime-green flowers. Each flower contains a few long stamens that splay outwards. These are carried, with their heads gently nodding, above a clump of very leathery, tooth-edged, deep green leaves. AGM. 60 cm (2 ft).

foetidus (Stinking Hellebore) Such an unkind name for a handsome plant. It is a native of Western Europe and produces a thick mound of dark green leaves that are deeply divided into pointed fingers. In spring, thick clusters of small, soft green, ball-like flowers emerge, each rimmed with purple. These open into small nodding cups. It is a variety that will self-seed. AGM. 90 cm (3 ft).

foetidus 'Wester Flisk' A highly decorative form of *H. foetidus* with grey-green foliage and stems heavily tinted with maroon. The flowers are soft green. 75 cm (2½ft).

niger (Christmas Rose) Short, strong stems bear open flowers of creamy white with a prominent cluster of yellow stamens. The flowers nod gently above broadly divided, dark green leaves. This variety is not very evergreen and needs good conditions to perform at its best, which makes it the least satisfactory of hellebores. AGM. 45 cm (18 in).

orientalis (Lenten Rose) In recent years, there has been a lot of interest in selecting variants of this plant. As a consequence the choice of flower shape and colour has increased dramatically. However, these are still cup-shaped and produced in shades of white or purple. The flowers are nearly always beautifully speckled inside with maroon and carried in clusters on branched stems. Its foliage is long and fingered and increases once the flowers fade. This is perhaps the most beautiful of all hellebores, but try to buy them while in flower, as they are often propagated from seed. 45 cm (18 in).

Helleborus foetidus

Helleborus foetidus 'Wester Flisk'

Helleborus orientalis

Hemerocallis 'Berlin Red'

Hemerocallis 'Bonanza'

HEMEROCALLIS
(Daylily)

I find it sad that daylilies are not more widely grown in Britain today. They are one of the most indestructible of perennials. Tall, upright stems are topped with clusters of large, colourful, often highly scented flowers. Each bloom lasts only a day, but many more buds are produced, opening in quick succession. There was a time when daylilies could be found only in trumpet formation and in colours of yellow, orange or red. However, with the recent, very active hybridisation by breeders in America and Europe, many new variations have been introduced. The flowers now range in shape from thin trumpets to flat, *Hibiscus*-like blooms and the colour from near white to rich purple. They are excellent for planting in large groups or mixing in borders. Their long, strap-shaped leaves form a dense clump that is perfect for weed-excluding ground cover. As for cultivation, they can be left undivided for many years and will grow in any soil, short of bog, in sun or shade.

'Berlin Red' Silky, red trumpets with pale ribs down the centre of the petals and dark green leaves. AGM. Midsummer. 90 cm (3 ft).

'Bonanza' A reliable plant with starry flowers of soft orange, each petal heavily marked with red. Midsummer. 90 cm (3 ft).

'Cartwheels' An aptly named plant with round, almost flat, golden yellow flowers. These are borne in clusters on long stems and are produced for weeks. AGM. Midsummer. 90 cm (3 ft).

'Catherine Woodbery' One of the prettiest daylilies and one that blooms for a long time. Its trumpet-shaped flowers are a delicate pink with just a hint of lavender. Midsummer. 90 cm (3 ft).

Hemerocallis 'Cartwheels'

Hemerocallis 'Catherine Woodbery'

Hemerocallis 'Chicago Picotee Queen'

Hemerocallis 'Chicago Silver'

Hemerocallis 'Cherry Cheeks'

Hemerocallis 'Children's Festival'

Hemerocallis 'Corky'

Hemerocallis croesus

Hemerocallis 'Diamond Dust'

Hemerocallis 'Double Daffodil'

'Cherry Cheeks' A handsome flaring, trumpet-shaped flower of smooth red-pink with peach-white backs to the petals. Midsummer. 90 cm (3 ft).

'Chicago Picotee Queen' A pretty plant with open, slightly scented, raspberry-pink flowers. These are flushed with maroon and have thick petals that are neatly pinched around the edges. The whole flower is covered with a sparkling sheen. I like to grow it with silvery plants. Midsummer. 75 cm (2½ ft).

'Chicago Silver' A distinctive flower that is Parma violet in colour. The petals are broad, pointed and neatly edged with white. This is a variety I mix with blue plants. Midsummer. 75 cm (2½ ft).

'Children's Festival' Little, orange-centred, trumpet-like flowers of soft apricot. Each petal has a pale mid-rib and curls back on itself. Midsummer. 45 cm (18 in).

'Corky' A small flowered variety with yellow, trumpet-shaped blooms. These have brown-backed sepals and are carried on slender stems. AGM. Early summer. 90 cm (3 ft).

croesus Star-shaped flowers of cinnamon, with yellow edges, are borne on long stems above slender, green foliage. It produces lots of blooms. Midsummer. 105 cm (3½ ft).

'Diamond Dust' This variety has large, open, very pale lemon flowers with broad, slightly ruffled petals. In hot weather it tends to pale to white. Midsummer. 90 cm (3 ft).

'Double Daffodil' A small-flowered variety with soft yellow trumpets. These are filled with a further ring of petals to form a gently ruffled, double bloom. Midsummer. 90 cm (3 ft).

'**Ed Murray**' A rather exotic, velvety flower with round, exceptionally dark claret-red flowers that are carried on long stems well above the foliage. Mid to late summer. 90 cm (3 ft).

fulva '**Flore Pleno**' An 'old' variety and arguably still the best double around. Deep orange petals are overlaid with red and form a loose, double, rosette-like flower. Midsummer. 105 cm (3½ ft).

'**Gentle Shepherd**' Large soft green buds open into lightly scented, creamy white flowers, with neatly puckered petals. When the weather is inclement, it can be shy to open. However, it is a strong grower and produces dozens of flowers, thus making it ideal for large planting schemes. Midsummer. 90 cm (3 ft).

'**George Cunningham**' A smooth flower of melon-orange that is borne on dark green stems above rich green leaves. Midsummer. 90 cm (3 ft).

'**Golden Chimes**' Small, round, golden yellow flowers with deep maroon backs to the sepals. These are carried on branched stems above an evergreen clump of leaves. AGM. 75 cm (2½ ft).

'**Grape Velvet**' A flower with small, round trumpets, the colour of crushed black grapes. These are neatly laced around the edges and have a velvety quality. Midsummer. 90 cm (3 ft).

Hemerocallis 'Ed Murray'

Hemerocallis fulva 'Flore Pleno'

Hemerocallis 'Gentle Shepherd'

Hemerocallis 'Golden Chimes'

Hemerocallis 'Grape Velvet'

Hemerocallis 'George Cunningham'

Hemerocallis 'Hyperion'

Hemerocallis 'Joan Senior'

Hemerocallis lilioasphodelus

'Hyperion' A most elegant variety and one for the traditionalists. Its highly scented, long, lemon trumpets are held on upright stems above beautifully arched foliage. Midsummer. 90 cm (3 ft).

'Indian Paintbrush' A plant that I have just discovered with rich orange flowers. These are wide and flat with ruffled edges and a yellow mid-rib to the petals. 75 cm ($2\frac{1}{2}$ft).

'Joan Senior' One of the best 'whites' to date. It has round, slightly scented flowers with thick, crinkled petals and a pale green throat. With age it deepens to very pale lemon. Midsummer. 90 cm (3 ft).

'Lemon Bells' This one reminds me of the true lilies. The perfectly shaped trumpet-like flowers are bright yellow and heavily scented. These are borne on long, well-branched stems with lots of buds to follow. AGM. Late summer. 75 cm ($2\frac{1}{2}$ft).

lilioasphodelus I prefer the old name for this beautiful flower, *Hemerocallis flava*, which is less of a mouthful than its newer name. This is one of the oldest known daylilies, and almost the first to bloom. It produces exceptionally fragrant, slim, lemon trumpets on slender stems above grassy foliage. AGM. Early summer. 90 cm (3 ft).

'Little Grapette' A variety that may take a little time to establish, but when it does, the flowers are small, round and of muted purple. These are produced in sprays on short stems just above a low clump of grassy leaves. Late summer. 90 cm (3 ft).

'Marion Vaughn' An elegant lily-like flower of deep lemon. These are fragrant and borne well above the foliage. AGM. Late summer. 90 cm (3 ft).

Hemerocallis 'Little Grapette'

Hemerocallis 'Indian Paintbrush'

Hemerocallis 'Lemon Bells'

Hemerocallis 'Marion Vaughn'

Hemerocallis 'Michele Coe'

Hemerocallis 'Neyron Rose'

Hemerocallis 'Pardon Me'

Hemerocallis 'Pink Charm'

Hemerocallis 'Pink Damask'

Hemerocallis 'Prairie Bells'

'Michele Coe' Round, evenly shaped peach-orange flowers, veined with pink and ruffled along the edges. The foliage is evergreen. Midsummer. 90 cm (3 ft).

'Neyron Rose' This produces purple tinted stems with wide, rich pink flowers. AGM. Midsummer. 90 cm (3 ft).

'Pardon Me' A delightful small-flowered variety with round blooms of rich red borne on slender stems. Midsummer. 45 cm (18 in).

'Pink Charm' An elegant variety with sprays of open, starlike, dark brick-pink flowers. These are carried on long, very erect, slender stems to form a rather airy plant. It is excellent for large planting schemes. Midsummer. 120 cm (4 ft).

'Pink Damask' One of the most popular daylilies. It produces an abundance of true lily-shaped, smooth, rich salmon-pink flowers. AGM. Midsummer. 90 cm (3 ft).

'Prairie Bells' A variety that is effective when planted *en masse*. Large clusters of round, rich pink flowers with petals that curl back on themselves. Mid to late summer. 90 cm (3 ft).

'Rootbeer' One of the darkest daylilies that I have seen to date. The flowers are neatly shaped, red-black, velvety and smooth, with a deep golden centre to accentuate their dark colour. Midsummer. 90 cm (3 ft).

'Stafford' A variety with perfect trumpets of rich red. These are brushed with black and have a deep centre of golden yellow. Midsummer. 90 cm (3 ft).

Hemerocallis 'Rootbeer'

Hemerocallis 'Stafford'

Hemerocallis 'Stella de Oro'

Hemerocallis 'Stoke Poges'

Hemerocallis 'Summer Wine'

'Stella de Oro' A little plant with small, bright yellow, trumpet-like flowers. These are produced for weeks above a neat clump of slim leaves which if not divided every other year will cease to produce flowers. I am not sure that it deserves the AGM it has been given. Mid to late summer. 30 cm (1 ft).

'Stoke Poges' Nicely formed trumpet-like flowers of lilac-pink, with an orange centre that is ringed by mauve-pink. AGM. Mid season. 90 cm (3 ft).

'Summer Wine' A stunning colour in any plant with trumpets of soft pink-purple, a deep lilac really, and lots of flowers. Mid to late summer. 90 cm (3 ft).

'Varsity' An open, round flower of very soft peach-pink with an inner circle of maroon. Midsummer. 90 cm (3 ft).

HESPERIS (Sweet Rocket, Dame's Violet)

Highly fragrant clusters of single, stocklike flowers are borne for many weeks on upright, leafy stems. These form a bushy plant that is ideal for cottage-style borders. It is a short-lived perennial that resents being pampered and therefore is useful for growing in a poor soil, provided it is well-drained and in sun. Late spring to early summer.

matronalis Soft purple flowers. 90 cm (3 ft).

matronalis albiflora White flowers. 90 cm (3 ft).

Hemerocallis 'Varsity'

Hesperis matronalis

Hesperis matronalis albiflora

HEUCHERA (Coral Flower)

These are plants that I have only recently
begun to appreciate. There was a time when
they could be found only with plain green
leaves and uneventful flowers. However, over
the last few decades many new varieties have
been introduced, mainly from the USA, and
now the triangular leaves, that form neat
mounds, come in an array of colours. Some
of the more useful plants are those with dark
leaves. All varieties produce upright stems
with small, bell-shaped flowers that are now
available in a variety of colours and sizes. I
use them in the front of a border, to knit
together a design of brightly coloured
flowers. They are well-behaved plants and
easy to grow in a well-drained soil, that does
not become too dry, in sun or partial shade.
Early summer.

'Chocolate Ruffles' This has a nice name,
but it is similar to the popular *Heuchera*
'Palace Purple'. It produces deeply cut,
mahogany-red leaves that are highlighted
with a sheen of bronze. Red stems carry
minute, dewy white flowers. 90 cm (3 ft).

'Green Ivory' A tough plant that produces
thick stems ending in dense panicles of bell-
shaped, greenish white flowers. The leaves
are mid-green. 75 cm (2½ ft).

'Helen Dillon' This will lighten up any dark
corner. Soft green leaves are liberally speckled
with white, almost obliterating the green. It
forms a thick mound with slender stems
carrying small, coral red flowers. 30 cm (1 ft).

'Palace Purple' A popular variety with
purple-red, bronze-burnished foliage. Its
slender stems carry frothy whorls of very
small, white flowers. AGM. 45 cm (18 in).

Heuchera 'Chocolate Ruffles'

Heuchera 'Green Ivory'

Heuchera 'Palace Purple'

Heuchera 'Helen Dillon'

Heuchera 'Plum Puddin'

Heuchera 'Strawberry Swirl'

Heuchera 'Stormy Seas'

'Plum Puddin' This produces large, glossy, deep plum leaves that are tinted with grey. From these, slender stems carry very small, almost non-existent flowers. 45 cm (18 in).

'Strawberry Swirl' Quite 'flowery' for a *Heuchera* with airy panicles of soft pink bells carried profusely above light green, ruffled foliage. 45 cm (18 in).

'Stormy Seas' One of my favourite varieties. Its ruffled, wine-purple leaves are heavily mottled with grey to give them a pewter sheen. Above these, slender red stems bear thick whorls of cream flowers. 45 cm (18 in).

x HEUCHERELLA

These are called *x Heucherella* because they are crosses between heucheras and tiarellas. However, I defy anyone, except a botanist, to spot the difference between these and their relatives. Like their parents, they produce neat clumps of triangular leaves and stems of small, bell-like flowers. As they are well-behaved, not travelling very far from the spot in which they were planted, they are useful for small borders. Grow in any well-drained soil that does not dry out, in sun or shade. Summer.

alba **'Bridget Bloom'** A mound of deep green leaves produces very slender stems with small, pink flowers. 45 cm (18 in).

alba **'Rosalie'** This has soft yellow-green leaves, which are heavily stained with red-brown in the centre, and flowers of pale coral-pink. 45 cm (18 in).

'Quick Silver' A mound of grey-burnished, brown foliage produces small, open, bell-shaped flowers with neatly fringed edges. 60 cm (2 ft).

x Heucherella alba 'Bridget Bloom'

x Heucherella 'Quick Silver'

x Heucherella alba 'Rosalie'

Hosta 'August Moon'

Hosta fortunei 'Albomarginata'

Hosta fortunei albopicta

HOSTA
(Plantain Lily, Funkia)

A stylish plant with handsome, architecturally useful foliage. The leaves form large clumps and produce, in gentle colours, long, straight stems with bell- or trumpet-shaped flowers. These are ideal for shady areas and for binding together a border containing a mixture of colour tones. Unfortunately, they attract one major pest – they are a delicacy to slugs. However, if your garden fails to attract frogs or hedgehogs (animals that simply adore these molluscs), there are one or two 'slug slaughter' methods. Try sinking a pot of beer into the ground as a trap, or sprinkling some sharp grit or egg shells around the plant. If these fail, purchase 'slug pellets' from a garden centre. Alternatively, some of the larger varieties look fabulous grown in containers as specimen plants. Grow in sun or shade, in a soil that does not bake hard during summer. Midsummer.

'August Moon' A yellow variety with rounded, deep yellow leaves that maintain their colour better in the shade. Pale lavender flowers. AGM. 45 cm (18 in).

fortunei This is one of the easiest varieties to grow. A lush, dense clump is made up of heart-shaped, deeply veined, matt green leaves and stems of violet trumpets. 60 cm (2 ft).

fortunei **'Albomarginata'** An easily grown, vigorous variety with shiny, mid-green leaves unevenly edged with a thin line of white. The mauve, bell-shaped flowers contain long, upturned stamens. 60 cm (2 ft).

Hosta fortunei

fortunei albopicta This is a variety that produces bright yellow leaves in spring. As they uncurl, they reveal an edge of plain green and by summer the whole leaf has deepened to mid-green. The flowers are lavender. AGM. 60 cm (2 ft).

fortunei aureomarginata Another variegated variety with heart-shaped, olive-green leaves edged with deep cream. It forms an open clump and produces lavender flowers. AGM. 60 cm (2 ft).

fortunei hyacinthina A handsome plant that forms a dense clump with long, pointed, grey-green leaves and soft lilac bells. AGM. 60 cm (2 ft).

Hosta fortunei hyacinthina

Hosta fortunei aureomarginata

Hosta 'Frances Williams'

Hosta 'Ginko Craig'

Hosta 'Golden Tiara'

Hosta 'Ground Master'

Hosta 'Halcyon'

'Frances Williams' When first introduced this was one of the most sought-after varieties. It is still one of the best. Very large, grey-green leaves form an arching mound. These are round, deeply veined, puckered and edged broadly with yellow. It retains its colour better in shade. The flowers are large, trumpet-shaped and white. AGM. 60 cm (2 ft).

'Ginko Craig' A low, spreading clump of foliage produces tall stems of soft purple trumpets. The leaves are slim, mid-green and edged with a thin line of white. 30 cm (1 ft).

'Golden Tiara' This forms an open clump with small round, soft green leaves, edged with lemon and sometimes white. Slim stems are thickly set with dangling lavender flowers. AGM. 30 cm (1 ft).

'Ground Master' A variety for smaller areas. Billowing whorls of deep lilac, trumpet-shaped flowers are carried on short stems above a creeping rosette of foliage. The leaves are long, pointed, wavy and white around the edges. 45 cm (18 in).

'Halcyon' This distinctly grey plant forms a compact mound with oval, heart-shaped, grey-blue leaves. Short stems bear stumpy spikes of soft lilac, bell-like flowers. AGM. 45 cm (18 in).

'Honeybells' A robust plant that is easy to grow. It has long, deeply veined, light green leaves and lilac flowers that are nicely scented. AGM. 75 cm (2½ft).

Hosta 'Honeybells'

Hosta 'Krossa Regal'

Hosta 'Patriot'

Hosta plantaginea japonica

Hosta 'Royal Standard'

'Krossa Regal' This is one of the most elegant hostas. Long, pointed, green-grey leaves are smooth, deeply veined and wavy around the edges. They form a handsome vaselike clump with pale lavender flowers borne on tall, upright stems. AGM. 90 cm (3 ft).

'Patriot' A bright green plant with oval, grass green leaves broadly edged with white. Large, light lavender, trumpet-like flowers are carried on tall stems. 75 cm ($2\frac{1}{2}$ ft).

plantaginea japonica One of the most fragrant hostas. It produces a large clump with round, deeply ridged, pale green leaves. The flowers are white, trumpet-shaped and smell strongly of hyacinths. AGM. 75 cm ($2\frac{1}{2}$ ft).

'Royal Standard' This robust variety forms a lush mound with broad, heart-shaped, slightly ruffled, rich green leaves. The flowers are white and trumpet-shaped. AGM. 60 cm (2 ft).

'Shade Fanfare' A plant that keeps its colour better in shady conditions. White-edged, light green leaves are paler in colour as they emerge. These form a neat rosette and produce soft lilac flowers. AGM. 45 cm (18 in).

sieboldiana Handsome, broad, grey-green, deeply veined leaves form a sculpted clump with white, lilac flushed flowers. 90 cm (3 ft).

sieboldiana elegans This is a classic variety. It has large, heart-shaped, blue-green foliage that grows into a dense, weed excluding mound. The flowers are lilac and carried in thick clusters just above the leaves. AGM. 90 cm (3 ft).

Hosta 'Shade Fanfare'

Hosta sieboldiana elegans

Hosta sieboldiana

Hosta tardiflora

Hosta 'Sum and Substance'

Hosta tokudama

'Sum and Substance' One of the biggest hostas and one largely rejected by slugs. The leaves are very large, round, deeply ridged and soft lime-green when young. As they age, they turn to deep yellow. Tall, grey stems carry lilac bells. AGM. 105 cm (3½ft).

tardiflora A glossy plant. Its shiny leaves are slim, dark green and form a low mound with mauve, trumpet-like flowers. 30 cm (1 ft).

tokudama An upright, slowly spreading plant with spoon-shaped, deeply veined, grey-blue leaves. It produces broad heads of white flowers. 45 cm (18 in).

undulata var. undulata A curly variety with mid-green leaves, heavily streaked with cream. These form a wavy mound that produces long stems of mauve bells. AGM. 30 cm (1 ft).

'Wide Brim' One for the front of a border as it forms a low, wide clump with mid-green leaves. These are broad, deeply veined and edged with a thick band of white. Lavender flowers. AGM. 45 cm (18 in).

Hosta undulata var. undulata

Hosta 'Wide Brim'

Houttuynia cordata 'Chameleon'

Inula ensifolia

HOUTTUYNIA *cordata* 'Chameleon'

A plant for gardens that have a wet area and a certain amount of shade. This is a slowly spreading plant that creates good ground cover with colourful, heart-shaped leaves. These are beautifully mottled with yellow and green, and streaked with red. Small, white flowers of great simplicity emerge just above the foliage. Midsummer. 15 cm (6 in).

INULA

These summery plants are irresistible to both bees and butterflies. They produce cheerful, slim-petalled, golden yellow flowers that are daisy-shaped in form. The foliage is variable, but can be invasive, so leave plenty of space around them when planting. Grow in a well-drained soil that remains moist during summer, in sun. Mid to late summer.

ensifolia Bright yellow daisies are produced on slender stems to form a spreading, open clump with slim, mid-green foliage. 60 cm (2 ft).

hookeri This is a soft plant with light green foliage that is furry to the touch. It grows into a low, spreading mound, producing furry buds on lax stems. These gradually release a swirl of petals that transform into a flat, finely rayed, bright yellow daisy with a golden centre. 60 cm (2 ft).

magnifica A majestic plant and a must for the back of a large border or wild area. Strong, upright stems, with large leaves, are topped with golden daisies that never fail to attract butterflies. 210 cm (7 ft).

royleana A large centre of yellow-orange is surrounded by a fringe of short, threadlike petals. These are borne in clusters on branched, upright stems with large, light green, heart-shaped leaves. 90 cm (3 ft).

Inula hookeri

Inula magnifica

Inula royleana

IRIS

These beautiful plants are grown in both hemispheres of the world, making them, perhaps, the most widely cultivated of all ornamental perennials. As a family, they are large and diverse, containing varieties for most conditions to be found within the garden; from sun to deep shade, from bog to well-drained sand. They all produce flowers with six, large petals and clumps of sword-like leaves. As there are literally thousands of varieties, both species and hybrids, it would have taken a whole book to do justice to this family. Therefore, to illustrate their diversity, I have chosen only a small number that I consider to be 'good garden plants'. To simplify matters, these have been divided into two different cultivation groups.

Iris 'Amethyst Flame'

Iris 'Annabel Jane'

BEARDED IRISES

Bearded Irises are probably the irises best known to gardeners. They are often referred to as 'Flag Irises' and sometimes, confusingly, called the 'Germanica Iris'. It is a flamboyant group of plants that contains the largest number of hybrids. These have evolved dramatically over the last 100 years as the number of varieties has increased. Where once only pale blue and purple were found, now pink, orange and black flowers are common. Where the flower shape was once gentle and elegant, newer introductions tend to be broad, ruffled and extravagant. However, these often survive better in windy, wet conditions than the older varieties. All are carried on stiff, upright stems that emerge from a broad clump of grey-green foliage. Bearded Irises can be planted in beds of their own, as they were in early parts of the 20th century, or mixed borders, provided their rhizomous roots are not shaded by other plants. They should be transplanted between late summer and early autumn in a sunny spot with very well-drained soil that is fairly neutral. If it is acid or wet, they will rot. In cooler climates be sure to place the rhizome at soil level, thus allowing it to be baked by the sun and to encourage flower buds for the following year.

Explaining the Iris

The following explains the terms used for the flowers: the 'falls' are the three upper petals; the 'standards' are the three lower petals; and the 'beard' is the caterpillar of hairs at the back of the falls. After each name a code is given in brackets. This traditionally refers to the flowering time and approximate height to which the plants will grow. However, for the purposes of this book, it refers to the flowering time only.

(TB) – Tall Bearded Irises flower during early summer.

(MB) – Median Bearded Irises flower during late spring and early summer.

(MTB) – Miniature Tall Bearded Irises are simply Tall Bearded Irises with small flowers.

(SDB) – Dwarf Bearded Irises flower during mid spring and late spring.

'Amethyst Flame' (TB) Gently ruffled flowers of deep lavender-blue with a hint of brown around the beard. 90 cm (3 ft).

'Annabel Jane' (TB) An elegant English variety with ruffled, lightly scented, lilac flowers carried on tall stems. These stands up well in adverse weather conditions. 120 cm (4 ft).

'Beverley Sills' (TB) At the moment there are very few good garden irises with pink flowers. This is by far the best with sweetly scented, coral pink blooms. 75 cm (2½ft).

'Blue Denim' (SDB) A profusely flowering small variety with neat, mid-blue blooms. 30 cm (1 ft).

Iris 'Beverley Sills'

Iris 'Blue Denim'

Iris 'Blue Shimmer'

Iris 'Bold Print'

Iris 'Bronzaire'

Iris 'Carnaby'

Iris 'Christmas Angel'

Iris 'Edith Wolford'

'**Blue Shimmer**' (TB) An older hybrid. Large, very sweetly scented, pale blue flowers with a speckling of white dots to the centre of each petal. 105 cm (3½ft).

'**Bold Print**' (MB) A prolific bloomer with white flowers heavily spotted and streaked with purple. 75 cm (2½ft).

'**Bronzaire**' (MB) Unusual, brightly coloured flowers with coppery yellow falls and golden yellow standards. AGM. 60 cm (2 ft).

'**Carnaby**' (TB) I think of this as being a very feminine flower. It has gently ruffled, lightly scented blooms with pink standards and purple-pink falls touched with buff. 90 cm (3 ft).

'**Champagne Elegance**' (TB) A twice-flowering variety with scented, ruffled flowers. These have white standards and peachy pink falls and produce a second crop of blooms during late summer. 75 cm (2½ft).

'**Christmas Angel**' (TB) A clear white flower, with a yellow beard, that produces ample quantities of blooms on strong stems. 90 cm (3 ft).

'**Edith Wolford**' (TB) A strange, but enticing combination of colours. Soft lemon standards and deep lilac falls that pale towards the edges. This is an extremely ruffled, broad-petalled flower that stands up well in wind and rain. 90 cm (3 ft).

'**Eyebright**' (SDB) Golden yellow flowers with eyelashes of dark maroon on the falls. This, like many dwarf varieties, was bred during the 1970s by the prolific English hybridiser, John Taylor. 30 cm (1 ft).

Iris 'Champagne Elegance'

Iris 'Eyebright'

Iris 'Gingerbread Man'

Iris flavescens

Iris 'Florentina'

Iris 'Godfrey Owen'

Iris 'Going My Way'

flavescens One of the so called 'species' irises that makes an excellent border plant. It forms thick clumps of foliage and sends up dozens of stems bearing delicate lemon flowers. Early summer. 75 cm (2½ ft).

'Florentina' (Orris Root) A plant to be found throughout the Mediterranean – even growing on traffic islands. Early in summer it produces scented, white flowers, heavily tinted with blue, that emerge from pale blue buds. AGM. Early summer. 75 cm (2½ ft).

'Gingerbread Man' (SDB) A dwarf variety with many ginger-brown flowers, each highlighted with a beard of dark lilac. 30 cm (1 ft).

'Godfrey Owen' (TB) Not a readily available plant but one I would not be without. It has large, perfectly formed, lightly scented, ruffled flowers. The standards are soft yellow while the falls are white and edged with lemon. 105 cm (3½ ft).

'Going My Way' (TB) A bold and clean flower. The standards are purple and lightly speckled with white in the centre. The white falls are broadly edged with purple. 105 cm (3½ ft).

'Honorabile' (MTB) This has small flowers of rich yellow, with falls heavily veined with dark maroon. It makes an excellent garden plant, producing lots of blooms. 75 cm (2½ ft).

'Indian Chief' (TB) A delicate, scented flower with maroon falls, pale red standards and a yellow beard. 90 cm (3 ft).

Iris 'Honorabile'

Iris 'Indian Chief'

'Jane Phillips' (TB) Introduced in 1950, this is still one of the best soft blue varieties with gently ruffled, sweetly scented flowers. AGM. 90 cm (3 ft).

'Jazz Festival' (TB) I am taking a gamble on this one. It is a new introduction which, to me, shows what iris breeders have been doing, as it bears so little resemblance to any wild iris. Despite this, it is an amazing plant. The petals are large, ruffled and fluted at the edges with broad, vibrant purple falls and soft peach standards. 90 cm (3 ft).

'Just Jennifer' (MB) The best white variety of its kind. It produces masses of purest white, ruffled flowers just above a thick clump of foliage. 75 cm (2½ft).

'Lilli-white' (SDB) A plant with pure white flowers. It is one of the older dwarf hybrids, introduced in 1957, but still one of the most reliable. 30 cm (1 ft).

'Meadow Court' (MB) An extremely free-flowering plant with dozens of yellow flowers. The falls are heavily flushed with maroon around a yellow beard. 45 cm (18 in).

Iris 'Just Jennifer'

Iris 'Jane Phillips'

Iris 'Jazz Festival'

Iris 'Lilli-white'

Iris 'Meadow Court'

Iris 'Olympic Torch'

Iris 'Ola Kala'

Iris pallida pallida

'Olympic Torch' (TB) This is a handsome plant with burnt orange flowers. A blend of different oranges makes the falls positively glow. AGM. 90 cm (3 ft).

'Ola Kala' (TB) A bright yellow flower, introduced in 1941, with a simple and clean shape that is carried on well-branched stems. 90 cm (3 ft).

pallida pallida This was given to me as 'Princess Beatrice', which I think is a far more flattering name. It makes an excellent border plant, producing thick clumps of clean foliage with lots of small, pale blue, lightly scented flowers. AGM. 90 cm (3 ft).

pallida **'Variegata'** A variety with handsome white-striped, soft green leaves and soft blue flowers. It can be slow to multiply. AGM. 75 cm (2½ ft).

Iris 'Provencal'

Iris pallida 'Variegata'

'Pledge Allegiance' (TB) A more recent introduction with perfectly ruffled, rich mid-blue flowers. There are many Tall Bearded Irises of this colour, but this is a strong variety that produces lots of flowers. 90 cm (3 ft).

'Provencal' (TB) A very handsome French variety with thick, velvety petals. The standards are almost entirely brown. Its falls are brown and speckled with white and yellow. 90 cm (3 ft).

Iris 'Pledge Allegiance'

Iris 'Sable'

Iris 'Ringo'

Iris 'Silverado'

Iris 'Snow Troll'

Iris 'Skier's Delight'

'Ringo' (TB) One of the most reliable varieties that I have grown. It produces extravagantly ruffled flowers with white standards and rosy purple falls, edged with white. 90 cm (3 ft).

'Sable' (TB) An older hybrid with velvety, dark purple falls and purple standards. At a distance, the whole flower appears black. 90 cm (3 ft).

'Silverado' (TB) Another modern but excellent plant. It has large, very ruffled flowers of the softest pale silver-blue I have seen. These are carried on very sturdy stems that admirably withstand inclement weather. 90 cm (3 ft).

'Siva Siva' (TB) A ruffled flower with bronze standards and white falls. The whole bloom is speckled with mahogany over a background of yellow. 90 cm (3 ft).

'Skier's Delight' (TB) A very new variety which is exceedingly beautiful. The flowers are lacy, ruffled, lightly scented and of the purest white. It has a white beard that is just touched with yellow. 90 cm (3 ft).

'Snow Mound' (TB) A perfectly balanced, modern variety. The purple falls are paler around the edges and its wide standards are pure white. 90 cm (3 ft).

'Snow Troll' (SDB) A profusely flowering plant with white standards and distinctive ochre falls. 30 cm (1 ft).

Iris 'Siva Siva'

Iris 'Snow Mound'

Iris 'Staten Island'

Iris 'Superstition'

Iris 'Supreme Sultan'

Iris 'Tall Chief'

'Staten Island' (TB) A 'traditionally' shaped, sweetly scented flower, from the 1940s. It produces round, ruffled, yellow standards and rich maroon falls that are finely edged with yellow. 90 cm (3 ft).

'Superstition' (TB) A dramatic black-flowered iris with undertones of purple to the shiny petals. The standards are wavy and the falls ruffled. AGM. 90 cm (3 ft).

'Supreme Sultan' (TB) A newer introduction from America with large, ruffled blooms. The standards are caramel and the falls dark ginger-brown. 90 cm (3 ft).

'Tall Chief' (TB) This produces quite small flowers for a Tall Bearded Iris. These are smooth and mahogany-brown. 90 cm (3 ft).

'Titan's Glory' (TB) An excellent plant. Scented, ruffled flowers of glossy, deep indigo blue are carried on very sturdy, short stems. AGM. 75 cm ($2\frac{1}{2}$ ft).

'White City' (TB) A scented, white variety from the 1930s with small flowers tinted with just the faintest hint of blue. 90 cm (3 ft).

Iris 'White City'

Iris 'Titan's Glory'

FINELY ROOTED IRISES

These are varieties that, unlike Bearded Irises, do not need their roots planted at ground level. Plant them with their roots sunk into the ground, like any other perennial. The varieties described here can be grown in a wide range of soils, in both sun and shade.

ensata A plant for the margins of ponds. Its large, flat flowers resemble floppy handkerchiefs and are found in shades of white, lilac or purple. They are borne on stiff stems above upright clumps of slender, mid-green leaves. Plant in sun or partial shade, in wet or very moist soils. AGM. Midsummer. 90 cm (3 ft).

foetidissima (Stinking Gladwyn Iris) This is one of the few irises that will grow in shade. A clump of dark green, shiny, almost leathery, evergreen leaves produces, during summer, rather unexciting buff-coloured, slim-petalled flowers. These develop into decorative seed pods that burst open during winter to reveal eye-catching red seeds. Grow in any soil that is not waterlogged, in sun or shade. Midsummer. 45 cm (18 in).

'Holden Clough' A hybrid iris with mothlike flowers of deep maroon, heavily striped with yellow. Mid-green, arching foliage forms a thick clump that tolerates a good degree of shade. Grow in a well-drained soil, in sun or partial shade. AGM. Midsummer. 90 cm (3 ft).

laevigata **'Variegata'** Slim, flat, purple-blue flowers are carried well above handsome yellow-striped, mid-green leaves. Although this is a water-loving plant, it will tolerate any soil that does not dry out, in sun. AGM. Midsummer. 90 cm (3 ft).

Iris ensata

Iris foetidissima

Iris 'Holden Clough'

Iris laevigata 'Variegata'

Iris sibirica 'Caesar's Brother'

Iris 'Monspur Cambridge Blue'

Iris pseudacorus

'Monspur Cambridge Blue' A very tall, upright plant for the back of a border with slim-petalled, soft violet-blue flowers. It can be grown in any neutral, well-drained soil, in sun. Late summer. 120 cm (4 ft).

pseudacorus (Yellow Flag) A plant native to boggy areas, ponds and streams. It produces, on tall stems, slender golden flowers with delicately patterned falls. Dark green leaves form an upright clump. Despite its natural habitat, I have found that it will grow in any soil, from wet to well-drained, in sun or partial shade. AGM. Early to midsummer. 120 cm (4 ft).

pseudacorus **'Variegata'** An attractive variation of the Yellow Flag. The mid-green leaves are striped with yellow and it produces the same golden yellow flowers. Like its sister it is ideal for moist soils, but can be grown in drier ones. AGM. Early summer. 120 cm (4 ft).

Iris pseudacorus 'Variegata'

Iris sibirica 'Flight of Butterflies'

Sibirica Iris hybrids

This is a group of valuable garden plants that will grow in any soil, from well-drained to moist, in sun to partial shade. All produce upright clumps with slender, mid-green leaves and stiff stems of delicate flowers. They can be planted near to streams or in mixed borders with soil that stays moist. Midsummer.

sibirica **'Caesar's Brother'** An intensely coloured flower of deep purple-blue with round falls and slim standards. 90 cm (3 ft).

sibirica **'Dreaming Yellow'** A rather flat flower with small, white standards and broad, flaring, creamy white falls. 90 cm (3 ft).

sibirica **'Flight of Butterflies'** Small, appropriately named flowers are borne on slender, long stems high above its foliage. The flowers have violet-blue standards and round white falls, perfectly veined with violet-blue. 75 cm (2½ ft).

Iris sibirica 'Dreaming Yellow'

sibirica **'Mrs Rowe'** A gentle plant with very small, pearly blue flowers borne on slender stems. 90 cm (3 ft).

sibirica **'Perry's Blue'** An older hybrid with bright sky-blue flowers. It has pendant-like falls that are delicately veined with ochre. 90 cm (3 ft).

sibirica **'Silver Edge'** One of my favourite varieties with ruffled, rich mid-blue flowers. The falls are finely edged with white. 90 cm (3 ft).

sibirica **'Sparkling Rose'** A robust plant with slender flowers of lavender-pink. 90 cm (3 ft).

sibirica **'White Swirl'** Pure white flower with flaring falls and slightly ruffled, upright standards. 90 cm (3 ft).

unguicularis A plant with many qualities, not least of which is that it flowers in late winter when almost all other perennials are asleep. Rather flimsy, delicately scented, pale blue flowers sit deep within a round clump of narrow, evergreen leaves. They are ideal for picking. Grow in any well-drained soil, other than bog, in sun. As a plant of North Africa, it is also suitable for hot, dry situations. AGM. Late winter. 45 cm (18 in).

Iris sibirica 'Mrs Rowe'

Iris sibirica 'Sparkling Rose'

Iris sibirica 'Silver Edge'

Iris sibirica 'White Swirl'

Iris sibirica 'Perry's Blue'

Iris unguicularis

Kirengeshoma palmata

Knautia macedonica

Kniphofia 'Bees' Sunset'

KIRENGESHOMA *palmata*

This most unusual plant, from Korea, produces sprays of waxy, soft yellow, shuttlecock-shaped flowers above a thick clump of maple-like, light green leaves. It is an ideal companion to hostas. Grow in a lightly shaded place, such as woodland, with a deep soil that does not dry out. AGM. Late summer. 90 cm (3 ft).

KNAUTIA *macedonica*

A highly worthy plant. Long-branched stems produce a stream of rich burgundy, pincushion-like flowers for a long period. In rich soils it will form a more upright plant than in poor ones, where it will grow into a prostrate clump. This is wonderful for mixing with other gentle specimens such as scabious, to which it is related. Plant in any well-drained soil, in sun. Summer. 45 cm (18 in) to 90 cm (3 ft).

KNIPHOFIA (Red Hot Poker, Torchlily)

These are plants to make a statement with, attracting birds that insist on pulling the stamens from the flowers as they open. This, however, does the flowers no harm! Erect stems are produced carrying pokers-like spires of tubular flowers. These open over a long period, at the bottom first, from buds of a different colour. At the base is a rosette of swordlike leaves that is, more often than not, evergreen. Grow in any very well-drained soil, including a sandy one, in sun. On heavier ground they may need some winter protection to prevent the crown from rotting, but once established they are exceptionally tolerant.

'Bees' Sunset' Bright tangerine flowers emerge from yellow buds on stems that are tinted with bronze. The foliage is slender and grey-green. AGM. Early summer. 105 cm ($3\frac{1}{2}$ ft).

'Ice Queen' An excellent plant in all respects, with broad spikes of cream flowers and green buds. Late summer to early autumn. 120 cm (4 ft).

'Jenny Bloom' This is a rather gentle variety with a loosely formed spike of slim, soft apricot flowers and cream buds. Late summer to mid autumn. 90 cm (3 ft).

Kniphofia 'Ice Queen'

Kniphofia 'Jenny Bloom'

Kniphofia 'Little Maid'

Kniphofia 'Sunningdale Yellow'

Kniphofia 'Toffee Nosed'

'Little Maid' A prolific variety. Slender stems end in densely packed spikes of soft yellow flowers and cream buds. It is excellent with grasses of a similar height. AGM. Late summer into autumn. 60 cm (2 ft).

'Percy's Pride' A free-flowering and robust plant with dense spikes of yellow flowers that open from lime-green buds. Summer. 90 cm (3 ft).

'Royal Standard' This grows into a vigorous plant with stout, dense spikes of yellow flowers and coral-red buds borne in equal proportions. AGM. Late summer. 105 cm ($3\frac{1}{2}$ ft).

'Sunningdale Yellow' A yellow-flowered variety with mid-green leaves. AGM. Late summer onwards. 90 cm (3 ft).

'Toffee Nosed' A gentle plant with conical spikes of loosely held flowers. These are pale yellow in bud and soft toffee-brown when open. AGM. Late summer. 120 cm (4 ft).

uvaria The well-known Red Hot Poker. Muted coral-red flowers open from soft yellow buds above whorls of grey-green leaves. It is almost indestructible when happily situated. Summer. 120 cm (4 ft).

Kniphofia 'Percy's Pride'

Kniphofia 'Royal Standard'

Kniphofia uvaria

LAMIUM (Dead Nettle)

These are perhaps not the most inspiring of plants, but it is a family that contains some of the most useful ground-covering perennials. All varieties produce upright spikes of hooded, large-lipped flowers that are borne just above dense foliage. If pampered in rich soil, they may become rampant enough to envelop other less vigorous varieties. Therefore, grow in a soil that is on the poor side, in sun or partial shade. Late spring into summer.

album 'Friday' A form of the European White Dead Nettle with handsomely striped leaves of yellow and mid-green. It needs to be grown in a soil that remains moist. 30 cm (1 ft).

galeobdolon 'Florentinum' (Yellow Archangel) An extremely useful creeping plant with spikes of soft yellow flowers and long, wandering stems of green leaves streaked with silver. This is an evergreen that will grow anywhere, including beneath conifer trees. 30 cm (1 ft).

garganicum garganicum A soft plant, both in flower and foliage, with broad clumps of slightly furry, grey-green leaves and large pink flowers. 30 cm (1 ft).

maculatum 'Anne Greenaway' Recently, a flurry of golden-leaved varieties has been introduced. Not all are reliably hardy, but this one seems better than most. It produces large, mauve flowers with attractive variegated foliage of yellow and deep green. Pull out any plain green leaves. 15 cm (6 in).

Lamium album 'Friday'

Lamium galeobdolon 'Florentinum'

Lamium maculatum 'Anne Greenaway'

Lamium garganicum garganicum

maculatum **'Beacon Silver'** Distinctive silver leaves form the background for mauve flowers. I have yet to see it without black markings on the leaves, which tend to spoil it. 15 cm (6 in).

maculatum **'Chequers'** A vigorous variety that is particularly good for ground cover. Large, soft purple flowers are carried above a dense mound of dark green leaves, just touched with white. 30 cm (1 ft).

maculatum **'James Boyd Parselle'** I consider this to be the best creeping *Lamium*. It produces a prostrate carpet of small, triangular, silver foliage smothered with short spikes of pink flowers. I grow this along the front of a border with *Ajuga reptans* 'Catlin's Giant'. 15 cm (6 in).

maculatum **'White Nancy'** I have seen this at Powys Castle in Wales, grown to great effect as a bedding plant around apple trees. The pure white flowers blend perfectly with its silvery foliage. AGM. 15 cm (6 in).

orvala Definitely the most handsome and largest *Lamium*. Unlike the others, which form creeping mounds, this produces a robust, upright clump with large, heart-shaped, mid-green, deeply veined leaves. Amongst these can be found very large, silky mauve flowers. It is ideal for a lightly wooded area. 45 cm (18 in).

Lamium maculatum 'Beacon Silver'

Lamium maculatum 'Chequers'

Lamium maculatum 'James Boyd Parselle'

Lamium maculatum 'White Nancy'

Lamium orvala

Lathyrus latifolius 'Blushing Bride'

Lathyrus latifolius 'White Pearl'

Lathyrus vernus

LATHYRUS

There are two distinct types of perennial sweet pea. One is a rambler producing its flowers in clusters on long stems, the other a low-growing, clump-forming plant. Both are beautiful, very ornamental and like a well-drained soil, in sun.

latifolius **'Blushing Bride'** (Everlasting Pea) Large, white, sweet pea-sized flowers are heavily flushed with pink and borne in thick clusters on long, branched stems. Allow it to ramble over a wall, hedge, or shrub, or down an embankment. AGM. Early summer. 180 cm (6 ft).

latifolius **'White Pearl'** (Everlasting Pea) This is like *Lathyrus l.* 'Blushing Bride', but it has clear white flowers. AGM. Early summer. 180 cm (6 ft).

vernus (Spring Vetchling) A charming little plant. This produces lots of small, vibrant purple flowers that sprout just before the rich green leaves appear. These are oval and pointed, and form a neat round clump. Once it has bloomed, the whole plant takes a 'back seat', so plant it in an accessible spot, perhaps near to the house. AGM. Early spring. 30 cm (1 ft).

vernus **'Alboroseus'** Very similar to *Lathyrus vernus*, but with pale pink flowers. These have white lower petals and the whole flower pales over time. AGM. Early spring. 30 cm (1 ft).

Lathyrus vernus 'Alboroseus'

Leucanthemella serotina

Leucanthemum x superbum 'Aglaia'

Leucanthemum x superbum 'Alaska'

Leucanthemum x superbum 'Horace Read'

Leucanthemum x superbum
'Phyllis Smith'

Leucanthemum x superbum 'Sonnenschein'

LEUCANTHEMELLA *serotina*

An elegant late-flowering plant for the back of the border. Upright stems carry toothed, fresh green leaves that form a dense clump. These are topped with simple, white daisies, each with a centre of yellow-green. Plant in a well-drained soil that does not dry out, in sun or partial shade. AGM. Early autumn. 150 cm (5 ft).

LEUCANTHEMUM (Shasta Daisy)

In recent years, the botanical powers that be have seen fit to rename all plants originally listed as *Chrysanthemum*. This has led to some wonderful tongue twisters, but *Leucanthemum x superbum* hybrids are those indestructible, large, crisp white daisies once listed as *Chrysanthemum maximum*. The flowers are carried on upright stems with deep green, serrated leaves that form a useful, slowly spreading clump. Still frequently found in gardens, they are wonderful for cutting and easy to grow in any well-drained soil, in sun or partial shade. Midsummer to early autumn.

x superbum 'Aglaia' A flat flower with slim, white petals, frilly enough to soften a centre filled with shorter, unruly petals. AGM. 90 cm (3 ft).

x superbum 'Alaska' This produces simple, single white flowers on sparsely leaved, long stems. These form an unpretentious clump that is ideal for placing towards the back of a border. 105 cm ($3\frac{1}{2}$ft).

x superbum 'Horace Read' The medium-sized, double flowers are shaped like flat, white pompons, with just a hint of lemon in the centre. 60 cm (2 ft).

x superbum 'Phyllis Smith' A decorative plant with a fringe of frilly, white petals unevenly placed around a yellow centre. 90 cm (3 ft).

x superbum 'Sonnenschein' A yellow-flowered variety (can this be a shasta daisy?) with canary-yellow buds that open into cleanly shaped, large, single, lemon flowers. Later these fade to soft cream. 105 cm ($3\frac{1}{2}$ft).

Leucanthemum x superbum 'T.E. Killin'

Leucojum aestivum 'Gravetye Giant'

x superbum **'T.E. Killin'** Clean white, semi-double, daisy-like flowers are produced in tremendous profusion. Each flower has a ring of short tufted petals that encircle its yellow centre. AGM. 90 cm (3 ft).

x superbum **'Wirral Supreme'** A flat, double white flower with a centre that entirely disappears beneath shorter petals. AGM. 90 cm (3 ft).

LEUCOJUM *aestivum* **'Gravetye Giant'** (Snowflake)

This is one of the few bulbous perennials to be included. It is a delight, bringing a touch of spring into a summer border, with tall, upright stems of dangling flowers. These are large, bell-shaped and tinged at the rim with green – just like a large snowdrop. Plant amongst low-growing perennials such as hardy geraniums in a well-drained soil, in sun or dappled shade. AGM. Early summer. 75 cm (2½ ft).

LIATRIS (Gayfeather, Blazing Star)

These rather unusual flowers are grown for the commercial cut flower market. Strong, stiffly erect stems end in a poker of round buds that open, at the top first, into fluffy flowers above a sparse clump of slim, mid-green foliage. They require a very well-drained soil in sun. Midsummer to autumn.

spicata Lilac flowers. 90 cm (3 ft).

spicata **'Alba'** White flowers. 90 cm (3 ft).

Leucanthemum x superbum 'Wirral Supreme'

Liatris spicata 'Alba'

Liatris spicata

LIBERTIA *grandiflora*

Sadly, this attractive New Zealand plant does not seem to have a common name. Perhaps it should be nicknamed 'White Butterflies', as this is what the small, open, white blooms look like. They are borne along smooth stems above a dense clump of long, slim, almost grasslike leaves. It is an ideal plant for a well-drained soil, in a hot, sunny spot. Once established, it can be left undivided for years. Early summer. 90 cm (3 ft).

LIGULARIA

These large, rather imposing plants are invaluable for moist soils, such as the damp area around natural ponds. They produce handsome clumps with large, round foliage, from which strong, upright stems emerge, bearing distinguished yellow flowers. They need a moist or wet soil, in sun or partial shade.

dentata **'Desdemona'** A handsome plant with round, rich green leaves that are a dramatic dark red underneath. These form a rounded clump and give rise to branched, mahogany-brown stems that bear clusters of deep orange flowers. In hot weather, if the soil is not wet, the leaves will droop pathetically. A plant for attracting bees. AGM. Late summer. 90 cm (3 ft).

'Gregynog Gold' This produces starry, orange flowers that open to form an impressive conical spike. These are carried on strong stems well above a clump of glossy, mid-green leaves. AGM. Late summer. 150 cm (5 ft).

hodgsonii A plant with flowers similar to *Ligularia dentata* 'Desdemona'. These are a softer orange and its leaves remain green. Midsummer. 90 cm (3 ft).

przewalskii A truly handsome plant with dark red-brown stems ending in elegant spires of small, starry, golden yellow flowers. It forms broad clumps with sharply toothed, mid-green leaves. This really does need a wet soil to perform at its best. Midsummer. 180 cm (6 ft).

wilsoniana Perhaps not the most widely available of ligularias, but one I really like. It produces tidy spires with starry, golden yellow flowers. These are carried on red stems above a mound of mid-green leaves. Midsummer. 120 cm (4 ft).

Libertia grandiflora

Ligularia 'Gregynog Gold'

Ligularia przewalskii

Ligularia dentata 'Desdemona'

Ligularia hodgsonii

Ligularia wilsoniana

Limonium platyphyllum

Linaria dalmatica

Linaria purpurea

LIMONIUM *platyphyllum*
(Sea Lavender, Statice)

Tiny, lavender-blue flowers are borne in a haze on wiry, multi-branched stems that just about hide the long, leathery, grey-green leaves. It is a late-flowering plant useful for hiding early-flowering varieties that, once the blooms are over, become rather untidy. It needs a very well-drained soil, such as sand, in sun. Midsummer to autumn. 45 cm (18 in).

LINARIA (Toadflax)

A long-flowering plant of European origin, which adapts perfectly to a border situation. These are rather refined and have upright, slender stems with little pointed leaves and small snapdragon-like flowers. They thrive in any soil, including poor, stony ones. Summer.

dalmatica Soft lemon flowers, lots of them, are borne on soft green stems. 90 cm (3 ft).

purpurea Incredibly slender spires of very tiny, rich purple flowers. These are borne on purple-grey stems with purple tinted leaves. 90 cm (3 ft).

purpurea 'Canon Went' This is a charming variation of *Linaria purpurea* with tiny, pink flowers and narrow, grey foliage. 90 cm (3 ft).

purpurea 'Springside White' An easily accommodated variant with pure white flowers, grey-green stems and leaves. 90 cm (3 ft).

purpurea 'Winifrid's Delight' I suspect that this is a cross between *L. dalmatica* and *L. purpurea*. It has small, yellow flowers, flushed with purple and blue-green foliage. 90 cm (3 ft).

Linaria purpurea 'Canon Went'

Linaria purpurea 'Springside White'

Linaria purpurea 'Winifrid's Delight'

LINUM *perenne* (Perennial Flax)

An unusual vase-shaped arrangement of slender stems, with small, blue-grey leaves that end in clusters of delicate, bright blue, saucer-like flowers. These bloom continuously throughout the summer and it is a useful plant for small borders. Grow in a very well-drained soil, in sun.
Summer. 45 cm (18 in).

LIRIOPE *muscari* (Lilyturf)

A tough little evergreen plant for slotting amongst low-growing perennials. Arching, dark green, grass-like leaves make a neat clump from which tight spikes of small, budlike lilac flowers emerge. It is well worth hunting down its attractive variegated form. Grow in any well-drained soil, in sun or partial shade. AGM. Late summer into autumn. 30 cm (1 ft).

LOBELIA

Unlike the well-known bedding *Lobelia*, the perennial version is a large, clump-forming plant. Erect, leafy stems are topped with colourful, large-lipped flowers that bloom for weeks on end. Being plants of wet areas, they can of course be grown along the margins of ponds and streams, but will adapt to any soil that does not dry out, in sun or partial shade. Summer.

cardinalis I know of only a few plants that produce such vivid red flowers. These are carried on deep red stems with deep red leaves.
AGM. 90 cm (3 ft).

x gerardii **'Vedrariensis'** A spectacular plant with large, rich violet-purple flowers and light green foliage.
90 cm (3 ft).

siphilitica A cheerful combination of bright blue flowers and light green leaves. 90 cm (3 ft).

tupa A dramatic plant. Long, truly scarlet flowers, each with an elongated, curling lower lip are carried on sage-green stems with large, soft green foliage. This is not reliably hardy, so grow it in a warm area of the garden.
120 cm (4 ft).

Linum perenne

Liriope muscari

Lobelia cardinalis

Lobelia x gerardii 'Vedrariensis'

Lobelia siphilitica

Lobelia tupa

LUNARIA *rediviva* (Perennial Honesty)

An upright plant with lush, mid-green, heart-shaped leaves and clusters of simple, lilac-white, highly scented flowers. As the flowers fade, they turn into large, transparent, flat, disclike seed pods that remain well into autumn. A useful plant for partially shaded spots, as well as sunny ones, in well-drained soil. Spring. 90 cm (3 ft).

Lunaria rediviva

Lupinus 'Chelsea Pensioner'

Lupinus 'My Castle'

LUPINUS (Lupin)

In my childhood, during the early 1960s, I can vividly recall fields of lupin. These were at Boningale Nurseries, near Wolverhampton, and a horse, pulling a plough, was used to weed through the rows of these handsome, somewhat old-fashioned plants. Sturdy stems of colourful, pea-shaped flowers form dense spikes above a lush mound of round, deeply divided, mid-green leaves. Most varieties found today are grown from seed and tend to be variable in both flower and quality. Therefore, try to seek out the varieties that have been propagated through cuttings. These produce better flower spikes that last far longer. In general, lupins are not long-lived, but their life can be extended if they are dead headed before the seeds develop. Unfortunately, in summer they are often smothered in an overcoat of white, woolly aphids. Try controlling these by spraying with an insecticide. Grow in very well-drained soil, particularly sand, in sun. Late spring into early summer.

'Alan Titchmarsh' A variety with perfect spikes of yellow flowers. AGM. 120 cm (4 ft).

'Chelsea Pensioner' Tapering spikes of rich scarlet with paler buds at the top. 120 cm (4 ft).

'My Castle' Brick-red flowers. A variety grown from seed. 120 cm (4 ft).

'Noble Maiden' Ivory white flowers. A variety grown from seed. 120 cm (4 ft).

'Olive Tolley' Rose-pink flowers with darker buds at the top. 120 cm (4 ft).

Lupinus 'Noble Maiden'

Lupinus 'Alan Titchmarsh'

Lupinus 'Olive Tolley'

Lupinus 'Rosalind Woodfield'

Lupinus 'The Chatelaine'

Lychnis chalcedonica

'Rosalind Woodfield' Apricot flowers opening from palest pink buds. 120 cm (4 ft).

'The Chatelaine' Two-tone flowers of pink and white. A variety grown from seed. 120 cm (4 ft).

'The Governor' Deep lavender-blue and white flowers. A variety grown from seed. 120 cm (4 ft).

LYCHNIS (Catchfly, Campion)

These are cheerful, easily grown plants with clusters of flat blooms carried on long, branched stems. They are excellent for mixing with other perennials, as they provide an extended and colourful display throughout the summer. Plant in any well-drained soil, in sun or partial shade.

chalcedonica (Maltese Cross) A difficult colour to match for sheer pureness. Its scarlet flowers are borne on leafy stems that can be rather brittle in windy areas. These form an upright clump with mid-green leaves. AGM. Midsummer. 90 cm (3 ft).

chalcedonica albiflora This has white flowers and grows like *L. chalcedonica*. Each flower is flushed with pink in the centre to give it a two-toned effect. Midsummer. 90 cm (3 ft).

Lupinus 'The Governor'

Lychnis chalcedonica albiflora

chalcedonica **'Flore Pleno'** A solid head of flowers with rosettes of double, scarlet blooms. It can be rather floppy when young, but after a while it grows into a sturdy clump. Midsummer. 90 cm (3 ft).

chalcedonica **'Salmonea'** Coral-pink flowers, edged with white, eventually fading to white. Like *L. c.* 'Flore Pleno' it can take sometime to look its best. Midsummer. 90 cm (3 ft).

coronaria (Dusty Miller, Rose Campion) This is extremely easy to grow. A basal rosette of long, soft grey-green leaves, coated with silver hairs, produces a mass of upright, well-branched stems. Each branch ends in single, flat, rich carmine pink flowers. Although short-lived, it will liberally self-seed. Grow in very well-drained soil, poor or dry. Summer. 75 cm (2½ft).

coronaria **'Alba'** A totally white plant – well, almost. Grey stems and leaves bear white flowers that are excellent for giving a little depth to a colourful border. It comes true from seed and is ideal for a dry soil. AGM. Summer. 75 cm (2½ft).

Lychnis chalcedonica 'Flore Pleno'

Lychnis chalcedonica 'Salmonea'

Lychnis coronaria

Lychnis coronaria 'Alba'

LYSIMACHIA (Loosestrife)

Useful if rather invasive plants for those who like perfectly balanced form, as neither the foliage nor the flowers dominate. They produce upright, leafy clumps with erect stems that end in small, starry flowers. If they get out of hand they are easily controlled with manual weeding methods. Grow in any soil that does not become too dry during the summer, in sun. Summer.

ciliata A perfect plant for warm colour schemes with soft green leaves and starry, cupped, gentle lemon-yellow flowers. 120 cm (4 ft).

ciliata **'Firecracker'** A stunning and unusual combination of clear yellow stars with chocolate brown foliage. The leaves are bronze as they emerge. A plant I grow with fluffy grasses. AGM. 120 cm (4 ft).

clethroides Long, slender stems terminate in tight, arching spikes of tiny, white flowers. These meld beautifully with its dark green foliage. AGM. 90 cm (3 ft).

ephemerum A stately plant with upright, waxy, grey-green leaves and stems topped with elegant, tapering spikes of pure white flowers, each with pink stamens. 90 cm (3 ft).

punctata A plant that needs to be kept under control in rich, moist soils. Bright yellow, cupped flowers are borne in whorls amongst rich green foliage to form an almost indestructible clump. 90 cm (3 ft).

punctata **'Alexander'** This is a variation of *Lysimachia punctata*, but not nearly as vigorous. Its yellow, starry flowers are almost lost amongst the drama of yellow splashed, green leaves. 90 cm (3 ft).

Lysimachia ciliata

Lysimachia ephemerum

Lysimachia ciliata 'Firecracker'

Lysimachia clethroides

Lysimachia punctata

Lysimachia punctata 'Alexander'

Lythrum salicaria 'Blush'

Lythrum salicaria 'Robert'

Macleaya cordata

LYTHRUM (Purple Loosestrife)

These hybrids of our European wild, stream-hugging native all form dense, erect clumps. Long, leafy stems end in slender, tapering spires of small flowers, which are carried in even rings. They provide a border with the kind of pink that is hard to find during summer, but demand a situation that remains moist, in sun or partial shade. Midsummer.

salicaria **'Blush'** A recent introduction with soft baby pink flowers. 90 cm (3 ft).

salicaria **'Lady Sackville'** Deep pink spires, thickly set with flowers. 120 cm (4 ft).

salicaria **'Robert'** Rich pink flowers carried in spikes. It is shorter than other varieties. 90 cm (3 ft).

virgatum **'Dropmore Purple'** A stunning colour; deep pink-purple flowers and deep green foliage. 90 cm (3 ft).

MACLEAYA (Plume Poppy)

A spectacular plant for growing at the back of a border. A clump of highly decorative, fig-shaped leaves produces slender, upright stems that carry airy plumes of tiny, almost colourless flowers. In tone these remind me of ladies' stockings. They need a soil that does not dry out, but is well-drained, in sun or light shade. Midsummer.

cordata A truly handsome plant with opaque, blue-green leaves and feathery plumes of buff-coloured flowers. AGM. 180 cm (6 ft).

microcarpa **'Kelway's Coral Plume'** Perhaps the most commonly grown variety with tiny, cream flowers and pink-bronze leaves and stems. AGM. 180 cm (6 ft).

Lythrum salicaria 'Lady Sackville'

Lythrum virgatum 'Dropmore Purple'

Macleaya microcarpa 'Kelway's Coral Plume'

Malva moschata alba

Matthiola perennial white

Matteuccia struthiopteris

Meconopsis betonicifolia

Meconopsis cambrica

MALVA *moschata alba* (Musk Mallow)

The native version can be a rather weedy thing, but tough, as this one is. It forms a bushy plant with round, finely divided, mid-green leaves and is covered for months with open, pure white flowers. It will grow in any well-drained soil in sun or partial shade. AGM. Summer. 75 cm (2½ft).

MATTEUCCIA *struthiopteris*
(Ostrich Fern, Shuttlecock Fern)

A delightful deciduous fern that forms an upright clump, shaped like a shuttlecock with long, elegant, fresh green leaves. It requires a shady site with plenty of moisture in humus-rich, preferably slightly acid soil. AGM. 120 cm (4 ft).

MATTHIOLA perennial white
(Perennial Night Scented Stock)

This is the only plant that I have included which does not have a proper title. It is too good to exclude and can be found in seed catalogues under this name. Pure white (or purple) flowers are borne in large, loose clusters above whirling rosettes of long, linear, pale green leaves. The flowers are amazingly scented and it is ideal for a dry soil in sun. Summer. 45 cm (18 in).

MECONOPSIS

These beautiful, but choice plants can be fussy to grow. They naturally inhabit cool, moist situations and although short-lived, they will seed around with gay abandon if the site suits them. Grow in partial or full shade. Early spring to early summer.

betonicifolia (Himalayan Blue Poppy) This produces cupped, sky-blue flowers that have a silky texture. Each contains a ring of golden stamens with a prominent stigma and is carried, in nodding clusters, on tall bristly stems. At the base, is a rosette of long, toothed, mid-green leaves. In its first year, remove the flowers before they bloom to get a better, if final, show the following season. AGM. 120 cm (4 ft).

cambrica (Welsh Poppy) A delightful individual that can be found growing on stone walls and in damp spots throughout western Britain. Slender stems bear delicate, solitary, lemon yellow or soft orange poppies above a clump of deeply divided, light green leaves. 30 cm (1 ft).

Meconopsis grandis

Meconopsis x sheldonii

grandis Like *M. betonicifolia*, this produces sky-blue flowers, but these are larger. AGM. 90 cm (3 ft).

napaulensis This tall plant will lighten up any rather dull or shady spot. Erect, sturdy, branched stems are topped with nodding flowers of bright pink. The petals are like crêpe paper and it has large, soft green leaves. 180 cm (6 ft).

x sheldonii Incredible violet-blue, cupped flowers nod gently on long, hairy, light green stems. Seated inside each flower is a perfect dome of golden stamens and at the base, a rosette of long, mid-green foliage. AGM. 120 cm (4 ft).

MELITTIS *melissophyllum* (Bastard Balm)

This is a delightful native of European woodlands. It has large flowers, rather like those of a *Lamium*. These are white, dabbed with magenta on each lower lip and emerge amongst large, oval, mid-green leaves. It forms a slowly spreading upright clump and is suitable for a soil that does not dry out, in partial shade. Late spring to early summer. 60 cm (2 ft).

MERTENSIA *pulmonarioides*
(Virginia Cowslip)

A darling of a plant. Loose clusters of sky-blue, trumpet-like flowers are borne on waxy stems with oval, blue-green leaves. As a woodland plant, it requires a humus-rich spot, in light shade. AGM. Late spring. 45 cm (18 in).

Meconopsis napaulensis

Mertensia pulmonarioides

Melittis melissophyllum

Milium effusum 'Aureum'

MILIUM *effusum* 'Aureum'
(Bowles' Golden Grass)

A useful semi-evergreen grass which, in spring, sends up yellow leaves that by summer deepen to soft green. I allow it to wander amongst blue spring flowers while at its most yellow-green. Short stems produce soft yellow flowers. Grow in a soil that does not dry out, in sun or partial shade. Summer. 30 cm (1 ft).

MISCANTHUS

These are, perhaps, the most decorative of ornamental grasses available at the moment. They form upright clumps with long, slim, straight, mid-green leaves and handsome plumes of very small, silky flowers. As they are not invasive, they are ideal for mixed borders. Plant in any well-drained soil that is reasonably fertile, in sun. Midsummer.

sinensis **'Kleine Fontane'** This produces silver flowers in arching, wandlike sprays well above the leaves. As they open, the plumes of flowers become fluffy. 120 cm (4 ft).

sinensis **'Nippon'** A less vigorous variety with tight plumes of silver-purple flowers. 105 cm (3½ft).

sinensis **'Zebrinus'** An appropriately named plant with white plumes of flowers borne above rich green leaves regularly marked with bands of yellow. 120 cm (4 ft).

MOLINIA *caerulea* 'Moorhexe'

A soft grass for the front of a border. This forms an upright clump with narrow, grey-green leaves that turn russet-red in autumn. The soft purple flowers are produced in profusion. Grow in a well-drained soil, in sun or partial shade. Late summer. 45 cm (18 in).

Miscanthus sinensis 'Kleine Fontane'

Miscanthus sinensis 'Nippon'

Miscanthus sinensis 'Zebrinus'

Molinia caerulea 'Moorhexe'

Monarda 'Aquarius'

Monarda 'Cambridge Scarlet'

MONARDA

(Bergamot, Bee Balm, Oswego Tea)

These are handsome, upright, clump-forming plants for borders with a moist soil. There are many hybrids, all producing haloes of colourful, hooded flowers that sit neatly in distinctive large bracts above heart-shaped, mid-green leaves. The whole plant is fragrant and attractive to the smaller kind of wild life, which at the height of summer makes them very special. One problem, though: the foliage is attacked during damp summers by mildew. Grow in sun or partial shade. Midsummer. 90 cm (3 ft).

'Aquarius' Lilac flowers with dark green foliage. 90 cm (3 ft).

'Cambridge Scarlet' Deep scarlet flowers. AGM. 90 cm (3 ft).

'Croftway Pink' Pure pink flowers. AGM. 90 cm (3 ft).

'Libra' Rich rose-pink flowers and reasonably mildew-resistant, mid-green foliage. 90 cm (3 ft).

'Sagittarius' Soft lilac flowers that pale to white at the base of each bloom. 90 cm (3 ft).

MORINA *longifolia* (Whorlflower)

A delightful thistle-like plant that produces whorls of intriguing, slender, trumpet-like, white flowers. These are tinged with pink and dangle, suicidally, from spiky bracts on stout, upright stems. At its base is a rosette of long, glossy, spiky, mid-green leaves. Grow in a very well-drained soil that is not too rich, in sun. Early summer. 60 cm (2 ft).

Monarda 'Croftway Pink'

Monarda 'Libra'

Monarda 'Sagittarius'

Morina longifolia

NEPETA (Catmint)

These mainly bushy plants create a gentle haze that is useful for softening the edges of borders and to link colours together. They vary in their growth pattern, but all produce slender stems with oval leaves and small, tubular flowers. However, with the exception of one or two varieties, they are simply adored by cats. To prevent any feline from destroying them, spike the young plants with sticks – it may work. In general they are easy to grow in any well-drained soil, in sun.

x faassenii A low plant that is perfect for filling a border quickly. It forms a spreading mound with small, scented, blue-grey foliage. This is covered for weeks with long, arching stems of tiny, soft blue flowers seated in lilac bracts. It is ideal for planting with old and shrub roses. Early to late summer. 45 cm (18 in).

govaniana A delicate plant with tall, elegant stems of soft green leaves and long, tubular, pale yellow flowers. In hot weather its foliage may shrivel if the ground dries out. Mid to late summer. 90 cm (3 ft).

grandiflora **'Dawn to Dusk'** An upright plant. Tight spikes of pale pink flowers are carried in grey-purple bracts on long stems with large, light green leaves. Midsummer. 90 cm (3 ft).

melissifolia A monster amongst nepetas, but one that is marvellous for the back of the border or for spots that needs a large, yet genteel plant. Upright stems are dressed with grey-green leaves and spikes of small, blue, lilac-flushed flowers. Not strongly scented, therefore cat-proof. Early to midsummer. 120 cm (4 ft).

nervosa A low, spreading variety. Upright stems end in tight spikes of bright blue flowers and carry mid-green, crinkled leaves. Mid to late summer. 45 cm (18 in).

nuda albiflora A very erect plant, ideal for the middle of a border. It produces straight stems with dense spikes of tiny, white flowers. These appear from creamy buds above grey-green leaves. Midsummer. 90 cm (3 ft).

racemosa **'Snowflake'** A prostrate plant useful for the front of a border. Long, arching stems carry spikes of white flowers, tinted with blue and soft grey-green leaves. Early to late summer. 30 cm (1 ft).

Nepeta x faassenii

Nepeta grandiflora 'Dawn to Dusk'

Nepeta melissifolia

Nepeta nuda albiflora

Nepeta govaniana

Nepeta nervosa

Nepeta racemosa 'Snowflake'

Nepeta sibirica 'Souvenir d'André Chaudron'

Nepeta 'Six Hills Giant'

Oenothera macrocarpa

sibirica **'Souvenir d'André Chaudron'** A rather rampant plant that needs to be placed where straying won't matter. Straight, slender stems bear thin, large-lipped, indigo-blue flowers with mint scented, grey-green leaves. Summer. 90 cm (3 ft).

'Six Hills Giant' An elegant, drifting sort of plant. A large clump is created from long stems of small, grey-green leaves and spikes of little, true blue flowers, which are seated in violet bracts. It looks at its best in large borders or on top of a retaining wall, where it will gently cascade over the edge. 120 cm (4 ft).

NERINE *bowdenii*

This is perhaps the hardiest and most commonly grown variety of these delightful South African bulbous perennials. A few long, lax leaves suddenly sprout in late summer, a short, spearlike stem that ends in a purse of buds. This bursts open to reveal a loose umbel of bright pink, lily-like trumpets. They require a warm spot with very well-drained soil, in sun. AGM. Late autumn. 60 cm (2 ft).

OENOTHERA
(Evening Primrose, Sundrops)

A varied group of plants, all with slim, deep green leaves and cupped flowers that bloom for weeks. The growth can be spreading and low, or tall and upright. Smaller varieties are useful for growing at the front of a border. The taller ones can be allowed to march around the garden as they tend to seed themselves about. Plant in any well-drained soil, including poor, in sun. Mid to late summer.

fruticosa **'Fyrverkeri'** This produces cupped, golden yellow flowers that emerge from red-tinted buds. These are borne in clusters, on upright stems, amongst bronze-tinted leaves and form a loose, relaxed clump. AGM. 45 cm (18 in).

macrocarpa (Ozark Sundrops) A low-growing plant for the front of a border. The prostrate stems, covered with narrow leaves, end in solitary, large, canary-yellow flowers. AGM. 23 cm (9 in).

speciosa **'Siskiyou'** A delicate variety with soft pink and white flowers, each with a bright yellow centre. These are carried individually on short, slender stems with long, light green leaves. 30 cm (1 ft).

Nerine bowdenii

Oenothera fruticosa 'Fyrverkeri'

Oenothera speciosa 'Siskiyou'

Oenothera stricta

Oenothera versicolor

Omphalodes cappadocica 'Starry Eyes'

Onopordon acanthium

stricta A tall, upright plant with bowl-shaped, lemon-scented, soft yellow blooms. These appear at regular intervals up red-green stems above a basal rosette of slender, deep green leaves. It is a short-lived plant that freely seeds itself around. 90 cm (3 ft).

versicolor This produces most unusual coloured flowers of tangerine, that turn vermilion with age. These emerge, in clusters, on erect stems among slim, jagged-edged, mid-green leaves. It is a plant well worth including for its beautiful colour. 90 cm (3 ft).

OMPHALODES (Navelwort)

A low-growing, clumping sort of plant, rather like a forget-me-not. It needs a cool shady spot, such as dappled woodland where it will add a little brightness. Spring.

cappadocica **'Starry Eyes'** A mass of soft blue flowers, edged with white to highlight the blue, is borne just above mid-green, heart-shaped leaves. 25 cm (10 in).

verna (Creeping Forget-me-not) Spreading, pointed, oval leaves form a background to little sprays of small, bright blue flowers. 25 cm (10 in).

ONOPORDON *acanthium*
(Scotch Thistle)

A tall and imposing plant that produces long, white, felted leaves, pricked around the edges in the manner of a thistle. From these arise very upright stems that are topped with large, thistle-like, soft purple flowers. As it is a biennial, it will die after flowering in the second year, so allow it to set seed. However, this is an immensely useful plant for the back of a border or for growing as a centrepiece plant. Grow in any very well-drained soil, in sun. Summer. 300 cm (10 ft).

Omphalodes verna

OPHIOPOGON *planiscapus* 'Nigrescens'

A unique plant that is similar to a grass. Thin, leathery, black, evergreen leaves produce tufts that gently leap around the ground and short, black stems of lilac-pink flowers, held like bunches of grapes. This slow-growing plant is effective when mixed with spring flowers, such as *Valeriana phu* 'Aurea', *Milium effusum* 'Aureum' or pulmonarias. Plant in a well-drained soil in sun or partial shade. AGM. Midsummer. 23 cm (9 in).

ORIGANUM (Marjoram)

A herb that is ever so useful for growing along the edges of borders, in pots and among paving. It forms tight hummocks with small, highly scented leaves that, when crushed, effuse a delicious scent. Later, it sends up slender stems with clusters of tiny flowers that attract bees and butterflies. Grow in a well-drained soil, preferably poor, in sun. Summer.

laevigatum 'Herrenhausen' A prolific variety. It produces erect stems with clusters of tiny, mauve flowers, maroon in bud. The round leaves are mid-green. AGM. 60 cm (2 ft).

laevigatum 'Hopley's' Slender, maroon stems bear short spikes of tiny, mauve flowers that emerge from maroon bracts above deep green leaves. 60 cm (2 ft).

OSMUNDA *regalis* (Royal Fern)

A majestic, large-leaved, deciduous fern with broad, upright fronds of soft, matt, mid-green that eventually grow into a large, slowly spreading clump. The young leaves are bronze as they unfurl in spring, becoming ochre in autumn. When it flowers, the spikes are dense, upright and coppery brown. Plant in a moist spot, such as the edge of a pond, in sun or partial shade. AGM. 120 cm (4 ft).

PACHYSANDRA *terminalis*

An evergreen perennial that is useful as a ground-cover plant in shady spots. It produces a waxy carpet of dark green leaves, lighter in colour when young, and spikes of little, white, petal-less flowers. There is a variegated version, which is not as hefty, and has white, margined, grey-green leaves. Grow in any moist soil, in partial or deep shade. AGM. Early summer. 23 cm (9 in).

Ophiopogon planiscapus 'Nigrescens'

Origanum laevigatum 'Herrenhausen'

Origanum laevigatum 'Hopley's'

Osmunda regalis

Pachysandra terminalis

PAEONIA
(Peony)

The herbaceous peony, as ancient as it is, is the most beautiful of all garden plants. Initially treasured by the Chinese for both its beauty and medicinal properties, it was discovered by Europeans after many centuries. It was developed further by French and English nurserymen during Victorian times, and it is now the Americans who, for the past hundred years, continue to breed these oriental beauties. These are classic border plants, but they unfortunately possess one fault. Their period of flowering, although dramatic, can be short. To compensate for this, they produce a fine clump of deeply divided foliage that is attractive from the moment its succulent shoots appear in spring, until autumn tints the leaves. Peonies are valuable border plants that combine wonderfully with many other perennials, including foxgloves, hardy geraniums and irises. Once established, they are easy to grow and are the longest lived of all herbaceous perennials. To illustrate this, I have included the date of introduction, if known, for each variety.

Cultivation

Peonies require a balanced, well-drained soil in sun, but will tolerate a little shade. When planting, be sure to place the eyes (leaf shoots) no more than an inch below the surface of the soil, otherwise the plant may fail to bloom. I am frequently asked by customers why peonies do not flower? The answer lies in one of the following reasons. Is it planted too deeply? Is it in shade? Is the soil too dry or does it have peony wilt ? The solution to all, except the last, is to lift the plant during autumn and replant it. For peony wilt, diagnosed when the buds or stems appear mouldy, simply spray with a fungicide.

Explaining the flower

The flowers, as described below, are produced in the following forms. Single: these produce one row of petals that open out to reveal the stamens. Semi-double: these are varieties with two or three rows of petals. Double varieties have flowers with many petals. Japanese hybrids produce the most exotic flowers; these are similar to single peonies, but contain a large centre of ribbon-like petaloids. Petaloids look like slender petals, but are in fact sterile stamens. The guard petals are the large, outer petals that protect the bud.

'Albert Crousse' A free-flowering plant with gently scented, fully double, pale pink flowers. The petals are suffused with cream and flecked with crimson. These are borne on strong stems with dark green leaves. (1893). Early summer. 90 cm (3 ft).

'Alexander Fleming' A shallowly domed, loose, sweetly scented, rich pink flower with a central swirl of evenly sized petals, edged with silver and, occasionally, red. It forms a strong, upright plant with dark green leaves. Early summer. 90 cm (3 ft).

'Auguste Dessert' A semi-double flower of rose-pink. The petals are speckled with deeper pink and edged with silver. Midsummer. 90 cm (3 ft).

'Avante Garde' Single, smoky-pink petals form a gentle cup around a large cluster of delicate golden stamens. A very early flowering variety that is carried on straight stems above round, shiny foliage. (1907). Late spring. 75 cm (2½ft).

Paeonia 'Albert Crousse'

Paeonia 'Alexander Fleming'

Paeonia 'Auguste Dessert'

Paeonia 'Avante Garde'

Paeonia 'Barbara'

Paeonia 'Blush Queen'

Paeonia 'Bowl of Beauty'

Paeonia 'Bowl of Cream'

Paeonia 'Buckeye Belle'

Paeonia 'Charm'

'Barbara' Double, perfectly domed, deep pink flowers, which soften in colour as they age. These are borne in profusion but are, unfortunately, scentless. However, they make excellent cut flowers. The leaves are deep green and crinkled. Early summer. 90 cm (3 ft).

'Blush Queen' Large, creamy white, lightly scented, double blooms are perfectly shaped like an old rose. These are tinted with pink in the centre and on the outer petals. A free-flowering, robust plant that is excellent for cutting. (1949). Early summer. 90 cm (3 ft).

'Bowl of Beauty' A scented Japanese type with large, bright pink guard petals and a centre of pale lemon, ribbon-like petaloids. The origin of this popular variety is unknown, but I suspect it is an old hybrid introduced directly from China. AGM. Early summer. 105 cm (3½ ft).

'Bowl of Cream' An early flowering hybrid with large, smooth, scented and very double, creamy white flowers. Each petal curves inwards to form a bowl that reveals a few yellow stamens. The foliage is grey-green and it makes a good cut flower. Late spring. 90 cm (3 ft).

'Buckeye Belle' Shallowly cupped flowers of very deep red with golden stamens. The petals are velvety, crinkled and tinged with brown and purple. This is one of the most beautiful plants for a spring border. (1956). Late spring. 90 cm (3 ft).

'Charm' A heavily scented Japanese flower with satiny petals of deep blood red. These open to reveal a bunch of lacy, crinkled red petaloids that are edged pale yellow. Carried on long, upright stems, it is one of the last to bloom. (1955). Early summer. 90 cm (3 ft).

Paeonia 'Claire de Lune'

Paeonia 'Duchesse de Nemours'

Paeonia 'Doreen'

'Claire de Lune' A delightful, very early variety with sweetly scented, pale lemon single flowers and an abundance of delicate, yellow stamens. These are balanced on red stems above a large, deep green bush of leaves. (1954). Late spring into early summer. 90 cm (3 ft).

'Doreen' A heavily scented Japanese variety with broad outer petals of fuchsia pink and a low, fluffy mound of frilly, golden yellow petaloids. It has strong red stems and glossy leaves, and it flowers later than most. (1940). Early summer. 90 cm (3 ft).

'Duchesse de Nemours' One of the oldest named hybrids with scented, loosely globular flowers of pure white, tinted with yellow at the base of the petals. By today's standards the flowers are small, but it is still one of the most widely grown white varieties. (1856). AGM. Early summer. 90 cm (3 ft).

'Edulis Superba' Probably the oldest hybrid peony still in cultivation. It produces a ball-like flower of rich pink. The petals curl inwards and are surrounded by large guard petals that are highlighted at the edges with silver. It smells just like old roses. (1824). Early summer. 105 cm ($3\frac{1}{2}$ft).

'Felix Crousse' A large, inner ball of uneven, purple-crimson petals is surrounded by larger guard petals and carried on arching stems. (1881). AGM. Early summer. 90 cm (3 ft).

'Festiva Maxima' Very pale pink buds open into scented, fully double, rather shaggy flowers of creamy white. These are tinted in the centre with blush pink and surrounded by large, outer guard petals that are sometimes flecked with red. (1851). AGM. Early summer. 90 cm (3 ft).

Paeonia 'Edulis Superba'

Paeonia 'Felix Crousse'

Paeonia 'Festiva Maxima'

Paeonia 'Flame'

Paeonia 'Gay Paree'

'**Flame**' A single variety with delicate, cupped petals of silky, bright pink. As the flowers age, they become soft red. These are carried on upright stems above large, bright green foliage. (1939). Early summer. 90 cm (3 ft).

'**Gay Paree**' This produces unusual Japanese-type flowers. They are two-toned; the guard petals are rich rose-pink and have a centre of soft cream petaloids that are tipped with pink. (1933). Early summer. 90 cm (3 ft).

'**Gilbert Barthelot**' A strongly scented, very double, domed flower of deep rose-pink. It is an excellent cut flower as well as a good garden plant. (1931). Early summer. 90 cm (3 ft).

'**Illini Belle**' A very dark red, almost black-red, semi-double, glossy flower with interwoven petals and yellow stamens. It is lightly scented. (1941). Late spring. 75 cm (2½ ft).

'**Kansas**' Large, double, distinctively coloured flowers of rich, clear, pink-red flowers, which are compact and frilly. These are carried on upright stems above a robust, leafy clump of foliage and are excellent for cutting. (1940). Early summer. 90 cm (3 ft).

'**Lady Alexandra Duff**' A strongly scented variety with semi-double, blush pink flowers and white central petals. (1902). AGM. Early summer. 90 cm (3 ft).

Paeonia 'Gilbert Barthelot'

Paeonia 'Lady Alexandra Duff'

Paeonia 'Illini Belle'

Paeonia 'Kansas'

Paeonia 'Laura Dessert'

Paeonia 'Lotus Queen'

Paeonia 'Miss America'

'Laura Dessert' One of the few yellow herbaceous peonies. The scented blooms, when young, open to reveal a frilly mound of slim, lemon petals. These pale with age into a dome of white that is surrounded by a row of white guard petals. The leaves are very dark green. (1913). AGM. Early summer. 75 cm (2½ ft).

'Lotus Queen' A Japanese flower with large, scented, white petals and soft yellow petaloids that fade to white with age. These are carried above a light green, bushy dome of foliage. (1947). Late spring. 90 cm (3 ft).

'Miss America' A handsome semi-double, scented, white flower opening from pink buds. Its petals are perfectly cupped around a centre of rich yellow stamens. (1936). Early summer. 90 cm (3 ft).

'Mister Ed' A very double, scented, ball-like, soft pink flower with a ruff of round, guard petals. The slender inner petals fade to white with age. As a sport of *P.* 'Monsieur Jules Elie', it may, like its partner, need staking. (1980). Early summer. 105 cm (3½ ft).

mollis This is an excellent, very early flowering perennial. It has delicate, lightly scented, single, cerise-pink flowers that contrast beautifully against its soft grey-green foliage. It is an ideal plant for small borders. Mid spring. 45 cm (18 in).

'Monsieur Jules Elie' A rather lax variety with scented, large, domed, rose-pink flowers. The petals curve inwards and are edged with silver. These are carried on long stems above an open clump of light green leaves. (1888). AGM. Early summer. 90 cm (3 ft).

Paeonia 'Mister Ed'

Paeonia mollis

Paeonia 'Monsieur Jules Elie'

Paeonia 'Mother's Choice'

Paeonia 'Mr G.F. Hemerick'

Paeonia 'Nymphe'

'Mother's Choice' A scented, fluffy, double white flower with interwoven petals and deep green leaves. It makes a good cut flower. (1950). Early summer. 90 cm (3 ft).

'Mr G.F. Hemerick' A lovely Japanese variety with bright pink guard petals and a large domed centre of pointed, crinkled, lemon petaloids. Its leaves are mid-green and crinkled. (1930). Early summer. 90 cm (3 ft).

'Nymphe' Deep rose-pink, strongly scented, single flowers are balanced, like saucers, on upright, red stems above broad, deep green leaves. (1913). Early summer. 90 cm (3 ft).

officinalis **'Anemoniflora Rosea'** This delightful, low-growing variety looks like a Japanese hybrid, but it is classed as a species peony. It has carmine pink flowers with broad guard petals that open flat, like a saucer. On this is seated a mound of thin, deep pink, yellow-edged petaloids. AGM. Late spring. 45 cm (18 in).

officinalis **'Rubra Plena'** To many, this is *the* peony. Still common in older gardens, it produces deep crimson blooms, packed with little rosettes of frilly petals. These are carried on long, lax stems amongst mid-green foliage. AGM. Late spring. 75 cm (2½ft).

'Pillow Talk' A delightful plant with tight, round, powder-puff like, double flowers of soft pink. These are scented and produced in abundance on strong, multi-branched stems above shiny, mid-green foliage. (1974). Early summer. 90 cm (3 ft).

Paeonia officinalis 'Anemoniflora Rosea'

Paeonia officinalis 'Rubra Plena'

Paeonia 'Pillow Talk'

'**Raspberry Sundae**' This glamorous hybrid is chameleon-like in habit. It produces a large, ball-like flower in pale ice cream tones. At first it is soft pink, with petals that curl inwards, but as it ages it opens into a fluffy dome with layers of cream and soft pink petals. The flowers are carried on short stems above deep green leaves. (1968). Early summer. 90 cm (3 ft).

'**Red Charm**' This is an excellent double, dark red variety that blooms for weeks on end. It produces a silky dome of slender petals that sit neatly upon a plate of large guard petals. These are carried on short, stiff stems above a clump of big, glossy leaves. (1944). Late spring to early summer. 75 cm ($2\frac{1}{2}$ft).

'**Reine Hortense**' A soft pink cup, flushed deeper pink at the edges, opens into a fluffy, double, soft pink flower. It is scented and held on strong red stems above mid-green leaves. (1857). Early summer. 90 cm (3 ft).

'**Sarah Bernhardt**' This is one of the most popular peonies for cutting. It is a tough reliable plant with long, branched stems of large, double, pure pink flowers. These are gently rounded and as they age, the petals pale at the edges. Late to flower. (1906). AGM. Early summer. 90 cm (3 ft).

'**Top Brass**' This is one of the more exotic hybrids, with a complicated arrangement of petals. In the early stages a tight white dome is seated on a ruff of large, white guard petals. As the flower ages, it opens into a frilly pompon with layers of slim cream petals, white laced ones and a flurry of erect pale pink petals emerging from the centre. The leaves are light green. (1968). Early summer. 105 cm ($3\frac{1}{2}$ft).

'**White Wings**' An excellent plant. A thick clump of mid-green leaves produces upright, well-branched stems with open, single, heavily scented flowers. These are white and translucent with a fluffy centre of fine, golden yellow stamens. (1949). Early summer. 90 cm (3 ft).

veitchii woodwardii Although not readily available, it is, for a species peony, reliably vigorous. A mound of pretty, deeply divided, light green leaves produces, if only fleetingly, small, nodding, single, rose-pink flowers. Mid spring. 45 cm (18 in).

Paeonia 'Raspberry Sundae'

Paeonia 'Reine Hortense'

Paeonia 'Sarah Bernhardt'

Paeonia 'White Wings'

Paeonia 'Red Charm'

Paeonia 'Top Brass'

Paeonia veitchii woodwardii

PANICUM *virgatum* 'Rehbraun'
(Switch Grass)

A colourful grass that grows into a slowly spreading clump. Upright leaves, deep green at first, become rich red by late summer. From this emerges erect stems of feathery, red-brown flowers. Try growing this with other richly coloured plants, such as *Sedum* 'Ruby Glow'. Grow in any well-drained soil, in sun or partial shade. Summer. 90 cm (3 ft).

PAPAVER *orientale*
(Oriental Poppy)

These are one of the garden's extroverts. On long stems they produce big, hairy buds that peel open to reveal a large flower with petals as delicate as crepe paper. At the centre of each luxurious bloom is an immense, velvety seed pod surrounded by a flurry of black stamens. The flowers are borne singly above a lush clump of rough leaves that dies back soon after flowering time. This allows other late-flowering plants to dominate, before they re-emerge during late summer. Oriental poppies are the toughies of the herbaceous world, surviving for years once established. However, although they are easy to grow, they do have one or two drawbacks. Tall varieties can be floppy and to grow upright they will need staking early in spring. Some varieties may seed around, thus diminishing what could be a prized collection of pink poppies to a sea of red. To prevent this, simply remove the seed pods as they mature. Grow in any well-drained soil, in sun or partial shade. Late spring and early summer.

'Beauty Queen' This produces tissue-thin, light orange, saucer-like flowers that bloom somewhat fleetingly, but there are many buds to follow. 90 cm (3 ft).

'Black and White' This is a spectacular variety with large, ruffled, white flowers. These are borne on strong stems with enormous black markings inside the petals. AGM. 90 cm (3 ft).

'Cedric Morris' This produces an attractive frilly flower of soft grey-pink, marked with maroon at the centre. AGM. 90 cm (3 ft).

'Curlilocks' A variety with large, daintily fringed, vermilion flowers. Unfortunately, it tends to be floppy in wet weather. 90 cm (3 ft).

Papaver 'Beauty Queen'

Papaver 'Black and White'

Panicum virgatum 'Rehbraun'

Papaver 'Cedric Morris'

Papaver 'Curlilocks'

Papaver 'Garden Glory'

Papaver 'Graue Witwe'

'Garden Glory' The is the most opulent flower I have come across so far. It produces very large, extravagantly ruffled, semi-double flowers of deep salmon-pink with a large black centre. These are carried on short, strong upright stems. 75 cm (2½ft).

Goliath Group 'Beauty of Livermere' An extremely handsome, rich red variety that produces its very cupped, black-centred blooms on very straight stems. These remain remarkably upright throughout summer. AGM. 120 cm (4 ft).

'Graue Witwe' A wonderful variety with large, petticoat-like blooms of palest grey-pink. 90 cm (3 ft).

'Karine' A gentle variety with shallow, smooth soft salmon-pink flowers, shaped like saucers. They are carried just above a low clump of leaves. AGM. 60 cm (2 ft).

'Kleine Tanzerin' A neat, short plant with masses of semi-double, salmon-pink flowers. These are ruffled, cupped and held on rigid stems. 60 cm (2 ft).

'Marcus Perry' A classic variety with large, red-orange flowers and black thumb prints at the base of each petal. 90 cm (3 ft).

Papaver Goliath Group 'Beauty of Livermere'

Papaver 'Karine'

Papaver 'Marcus Perry'

Papaver 'Kleine Tanzerin'

'**Mrs. Perry**' A delicate salmon-pink flower with black spots borne on long stems. This was the first pink Oriental poppy. AGM. 90 cm (3 ft).

'**Patty's Plum**' A flower of unusual colouring, which is not my favourite. It produces large, ruffled blooms of deep plum-mauve that often fail to open properly in wet conditions. The long stems also need staking. 90 cm (3 ft).

'**Perry's White**' An old and trusted variety with pure white flowers, emphasised by black at the base of each petal. 90 cm (3 ft).

'**Picotee**' A large, two-toned flower of white, edged with a broad band of orange-red. 90 cm (3 ft).

'**Sultana**' A rather lax plant with vibrant pink flowers. It combines perfectly with blue flowers. 90 cm (3 ft).

'**Turkenlouis**' A dramatic plant, it produces large, fringed, vibrant red flowers with a black spot on each petal and a big black centre. These are borne on strong, upright stems. 105 cm (3½ ft).

'**Turkish Delight**' This could be confused with *Papaver o.* 'Mrs. Perry', as it produces similar deeply cupped, pale pink flowers. However, these have no black markings and are borne on upright stems. AGM. 90 cm (3 ft).

Papaver 'Mrs. Perry'

Papaver 'Patty's Plum'

Papaver 'Perry's White'

Papaver 'Picotee'

Papaver 'Sultana'

Papaver 'Turkenlouis'

Papaver 'Turkish Delight'

PENSTEMON

These are plants more suited to bedding schemes than borders. Colourful, tubular flowers are carried on upright, leafy stems that form a largely evergreen bush. In recent years, the increase in popularity of penstemons seems to have matched the increase in warmer winters. Once hardy only in southern England, they are now proving tough in the cold English Midlands. I include here only a very small selection of the many hybrids that are currently available. All will grow in a well-drained soil, in sun. Summer.

'Apple Blossom' Slender, pale pink, trumpet-like flowers with white interiors and slim, light green leaves. AGM. 60 cm (2 ft).

barbatus Unlike the other varieties, this is a lax plant. Long, straight stems carry loose panicles of very slim, coral flowers with deep green foliage. 120 cm (4 ft).

digitalis **'Husker Red'** A handsome colour combination. Small white flowers, delicately flushed with lilac, are carried on dark red stems with leaves of the same colour. 105 cm (3½ft).

Penstemon 'Apple Blossom'

Penstemon barbatus

Penstemon 'Flamingo'

Penstemon digitalis 'Husker Red'

Penstemon 'King George V'

'Flamingo' Broad, rich pink trumpets with a white throat and mid-green leaves. 75 cm (2½ft).

'King George V' Bright red flowers carried on red stems. The leaves are mid-green. 75 cm (2½ft).

'Stapleford Gem' Large, yet slender, lilac-blue flowers, mottled with pink and mid-green leaves. AGM. 60 cm (2 ft).

whippleanus Forget its rather unflattering name, this is a very useful low-growing plant for the front of a border. Short spikes of soft plum-purple flowers are produced in profusion above a small clump of light green leaves. 30 cm (1 ft).

'White Bedder' Large, trumpet-like flowers of pure white are carried above soft green foliage. AGM. 75 cm (2½ft).

Penstemon 'Stapleford Gem'

Penstemon whippleanus

Penstemon 'White Bedder'

Perovskia atriplicifolia 'Blue Spire'

Periscaria affinis 'Superba'

Periscaria amplexicaulis 'Firetail'

PEROVSKIA *atriplicifolia* **'Blue Spire'**
(Russian Sage)

A graceful, slow-growing, open bushy plant. It produces slender, white stems and long, scented, deeply cut, white leaves with spikes of small, blue flowers that emerge from woolly bracts. Technically a subshrub, I grow this as a perennial and leave the stems uncut in autumn to provide structure throughout the winter. Grow in a very well-drained soil, in sun. AGM. Late summer to autumn. 105 cm ($3\frac{1}{2}$ ft).

PERSICARIA (Polygonum, Bistort)

These are not the most flowery of herbaceous plants, but bold foliage and short spikes of tiny flowers make them ideal subjects for combining with grasses and daisy-shaped blooms. The larger persicarias tend to be vigorous, producing useful mounds of weed-excluding foliage. All are easy to grow in a soil that does not dry out during the summer, in sun or shade.

affinis **'Superba'** A flat carpet of long, oval, rich green leaves produces erect stems topped with thick spikes of very small, bell-like flowers. At first, these are ruby-red, then turn to pink and finally to white. In autumn the leaves are richly coloured. AGM. Summer.
23 cm (9 in).

amplexicaulis **'Alba'** All *P. amplexicaulis* types are natural thugs, but this, in appearance, is unusually gentle. Oval, pointed, soft green leaves form a large mound from which many slender spikes of tiny, pure white flowers emerge. Each has long stamens to give it a fluffy feel. It looks extremely effective in autumn with asters. Late summer to autumn. 120 cm (4 ft).

amplexicaulis **'Atrosanguinea'** A sea of slender, arching stems ends in crimson spikes that are borne above a large mound of oval, rich green leaves. It needs space to perform at its best. Midsummer into autumn.
120 cm (4 ft).

amplexicaulis **'Firetail'** This is a robust plant with fine, red-pink flower spikes, broader than *P. amplexicaulis* 'Atrosanguinea' and large, pointed, rich green leaves. AGM. Midsummer to autumn.
120 cm (4 ft).

bistorta **'Superba'** A bold and handsome plant. A broad mound of large, soft green leaves, shaped like the wild dock plant, produces long stems with poker-like spikes of tiny, soft pink flowers. It can be rather invasive, but this is extremely useful for marginal plantings around ponds. Also grow it in moist woodland and borders. AGM. Late spring to early summer. 90 cm (3 ft).

Periscaria amplexicaulis 'Alba'

Periscaria amp. 'Atrosanguinea'

Periscaria bistorta 'Superba'

Petasites japonicus giganteus

PETASITES *japonicus giganteus*
(Butterbur, Sweet Coltsfoot)

A giant coltsfoot with red stems of little, round, fluffy flowers held in open spikes above broad, umbrella-like leaves. Beware, it spreads with vigour be used only in large wild areas. Grow in any type of soil that remains moist, in sun or partial shade. Early spring. 75 cm (2½ ft).

PHALARIS *arundinacea picta*
(Gardener's Garter)

I have no idea where its common name comes from, but once this grass enters your borders, it will strangle most of its near neighbours. Despite this, it is an appealing variety that forms a dense, upright clump with pale green, white striped leaves. Later, geometrically shaped spikes of white flowers are produced. Grow in a well-drained or moist soil, in sun or partial shade. Midsummer. 90 cm (3 ft).

PHLOMIS

These very handsome plants possess a quiet beauty and provide a summer border with strong, upright form. Both varieties are easily grown in a well-drained soil, in sun. Summer.

russelliana Architectural in habit, this produces large, hooded, pale yellow flowers that open individually over a long period. They are held in whorls on sturdy, velvety stems above big, evergreen, felted, heart-shaped leaves. It may take a year or two to establish, but when it does, it is a most impressive carpeting plant.
AGM. 90 cm (3 ft).

tuberosa A very erect plant with soft lavender, hooded flowers. These are carried in whorls on leafy, deep purple stems above a basal clump of long, serrated, deep green leaves.
90 cm (3 ft).

Phlomis russelliana

Phlomis tuberosa

Phalaris arundinacea picta

PHLOX

For decades, these have been one of the mainstays of the traditional English herbaceous border. An upright clump of stiff, leafy stems carries large clusters of simple, often very colourful, flowers. These are not my favourite plants, but they do have two good qualities. They are exceedingly fragrant and make wonderful cut flowers. Over the years, many varieties have been introduced and continue to be, which means, hopefully, that the old problems of eelworm and mildew will be eradicated. To perform at their best, they need to be grown in a very fertile, well-drained soil, in sun. Mid to late summer.

P. maculata hybrids
(Meadow Phlox)

Of the two types, these are the more elegant and tend not to suffer from debilitating diseases. They produce tapering spikes of small, flat, saucer-like flowers and long, pale green foliage.

maculata **'Alpha'** Mauve-pink flowers. AGM. 90 cm (3 ft).

maculata **'Omega'** White flowers with a delicate central eye of pink. AGM. 90 cm (3 ft).

maculata **'Rosalinde'** Rich lilac-pink flowers. 90 cm (3 ft).

Phlox maculata 'Alpha'

Phlox maculata 'Rosalinde'

Phlox maculata 'Omega'

Phlox paniculata alba

Phlox paniculata 'Amethyst'

Phlox paniculata 'Brigadier'

P. paniculata hybrids

Noted for their intense colour, these produce large, round heads of flowers with linear, mid-green leaves. Generally, to achieve their full potential, *P. paniculata* hybrids need to be grown in a humus-rich soil, in sun.

paniculata alba Loose heads of pure white. 105 cm (3½ft).

paniculata **'Amethyst'** Rosy lilac flowers. AGM. 90 cm (3 ft).

paniculata **'Brigadier'** Vibrant orange-red flowers. AGM. 90 cm (3 ft).

paniculata **'Europe'** White flowers with a carmine eye. 90 cm (3 ft).

paniculata **'Harlequin'** Cream and green variegated foliage with rich rose-mauve flowers. 90 cm (3 ft).

paniculata **'Norah Leigh'** Handsomely variegated foliage with disappointing small, pale pink flowers. 90 cm (3 ft).

Phlox paniculata 'Europe'

Phlox paniculata 'Harlequin'

Phlox paniculata 'Norah Leigh'

Phlox paniculata 'Otley Choice'

Phlox paniculata 'Prospero'

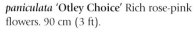

paniculata **'Otley Choice'** Rich rose-pink flowers. 90 cm (3 ft).

paniculata **'Prospero'** Soft lilac flowers. AGM. 90 cm (3 ft).

paniculata **'Sandringham'** Pale pink flowers each with a deeper eye of pink. 90 cm (3 ft).

paniculata **'Starfire'** Deep pink-red flowers with rich red-green stems and leaves. Not the strongest variety, but the foliage is attractive. 75 cm (2½ ft).

paniculata **'Tenor'** Bright carmine flowers with red stems. 75 cm (2½ ft).

paniculata **'Windsor'** Brilliant salmon-pink flowers with a cerise pink eye. AGM. 90 cm (3 ft).

Phlox paniculata 'Sandringham'

Phlox paniculata 'Windsor'

Phlox paniculata 'Starfire'

Phlox paniculata 'Tenor'

PHORMIUM (New Zealand Flax)

I am a great fan of these majestic plants. They form broad thickets with long strappy leaves which, in Britain, tend not to flower. When they do, these are long and tubular, like downward pointing beaks, and carried on stiff, branched stems. They are wonderful for providing architectural structure to borders, but resent wet, cold winters. Therefore, grow them in full sun, in a soil that is well-drained yet moist, but does not freeze. Late summer.

tenax **Purpureum** Broad, thick leaves of deep bronze-brown and dark red flowers. Its foliage grows to 90 cm (3 ft) while the flower stems can get to 240 cm (8 ft).

'Yellow Wave' A smaller variety with yellow foliage, delicately striped with pale green. AGM. Foliage to 75 cm (2½ ft). Flowers to 240 cm (8 ft).

PHUOPSIS *stylosa*

A spreading plant with pompon-like clusters of tiny, vivid pink flowers. These are borne in profusion above a thick carpet of linear, light green foliage. The leaves are similar to *Galium odoratum*, rough to the touch, held in whorls and scented. This rather untidy plant has one virtue: it flowers continuously. Grow in any soil, well-drained or moist, in sun or partial shade. Late spring to midsummer. 23 cm (9 in).

PHYSALIS *alkekengi franchetii* (Chinese Lantern)

The charm of this plant lies in the papery, bright orange-red, balloon-like covering to its fruits. These nestle amongst upright stems of lush, mid-green, heart-shaped leaves to form a rather untidy, spreading bush. It produces insignificant flowers of soft yellow, but the papery balloons can be dried for flower arrangements. Grow in any soil, in sun or partial shade. Midsummer. 90 cm (3 ft).

Phuopsis stylosa

Phormium tenax Purpureum

Phormium 'Yellow Wave'

Physalis alkekengi franchetii

Physostegia virginiana speciosa 'Bouquet Rose'

Physostegia virginiana speciosa 'Variegata'

PHYSOSTEGIA (Obedient Plant)

An elegant plant, with tapering spikes of tubular flowers held at right angles to the stems. I have not witnessed this, but apparently they remain in the same position when the plant is moved, hence its common name. It has slim, toothed, mid-green leaves that, with erect stems, form a gently spreading clump. This easily grown plant from North America will grow in any well-drained soil that remains moist, in sun. Midsummer.

virginiana speciosa **'Bouquet Rose'** Soft pink flowers. 90 cm (3 ft).

virginiana speciosa **'Summer Snow'** Pure white flowers. AGM. 90 cm (3 ft).

virginiana speciosa **'Variegata'** Pale pink flowers and white splashed leaves. 90 cm (3 ft).

PILOSELLA *aurantiaca*
(Orange Hawkweed, Fox and Cubs)

A native European wild flower found in grassy places. Clusters of flat, vivid orange flowers, rather like those of the dandelion, are produced for weeks on hairy stems. Long, mid-green leaves form a rosette and although it is short-lived, it liberally seeds itself around. Grow in a well-drained or dry soil, in sun or partial shade. Summer. 30 cm (1 ft).

PIMPINELLA *major* 'Rosea'

This gentle European native produces an umbrella of tiny, rich pink flowers. These are carried on short stalks above soft, much-divided, mid-green leaves that rabbits simply adore. Grow in any well-drained soil that remains moist, in sun or partial shade. Early to midsummer. 75 cm (2½ ft).

Physostegia virginiana speciosa 'Summer Snow'

Pimpinella major 'Rosea'

Pilosella aurantiaca

Piantago lanceolata 'Streaker'

Platycodon grandiflorus 'Blue Haze'

PLANTAGO (Plantain)

My interest in European wild flowers extends to the humble plantain, a plant that has been overlooked for far too long. These quietly beautiful plants produce rosettes of deeply veined leaves and short stems carrying small, tightly packed spikes of tiny flowers. They are ideal for poor soils or paving and should be grown for their architectural, if petite, value. Grow in any well-drained soil, in sun. Late spring into late summer.

lanceolata **'Streaker'** A beautiful plant with long, slim, soft green leaves, edged with cream. It produces stumpy spikes of brown flowers. 15 cm (6 in).

major **'Rubrifolia'** This is a handsome variety with large, rich red, deeply veined leaves and long spikes of soft brown flowers. It tends to seed itself around. 30 cm (1 ft).

PLATYCODON (Balloon Flower)

Buds, like upside-down balloons, burst into wide, cupped flowers with pointed edges to the petals. These are borne on short stems with oval, blue-grey leaves to form an open clump suitable for the front of a border. Slow to grow, they need a very well-drained, rich soil, in sun or partial shade. Late summer.

grandiflorus **'Blue Haze'** Very pale blue flowers; the backs of the petals are paler in colour. 45 cm (18 in).

grandiflorus **'Hakone Double Blue'** Rich, deep blue flowers with a further inner ring of petals. 45 cm (18 in).

grandiflorus **'Perlmutterschale'** Very pale pink flowers. 45 cm (18 in).

Plantago major 'Rubrifolia'

Platycodon grandiflorus 'Perlmutterschale'

Platycodon grandiflorus 'Hakone Double Blue'

PODOPHYLLUM *hexandrum*

A science fiction-like plant with a toadstool-shaped leaf bud, which bursts through the soil and opens, like an umbrella, into a camouflage-coloured leaf. Under this a solitary, soft pink, single flower emerges with five prominent stamens. It is suitable for moist spots in shade or woodlands, but must not to be eaten as it is highly toxic! Spring. 45 cm (18 in).

Podophyllum hexandrum

Polemonium caeruleum album

POLEMONIUM (Jacob's Ladder)

These have been grown in gardens for centuries. They are delicate plants, short-lived but ideal for less formal cottage-style gardens. They produce clumps of small, mid-green leaves in ladder formation and an abundance of small flowers. Easy to grow, they will thrive in a well-drained soil that does not become too dry, in sun or partial shade.

caeruleum Small clusters of open, lilac-blue flowers. Early to midsummer. 90 cm (3 ft).

caeruleum album Clusters of pure white, bell-like flowers highlighted with blue tipped stamens. Early summer. 90 cm (3 ft).

carneum A loose clump-forming variety with clusters of open, soft peach-pink flowers. Early summer. 75 cm (2½ft).

'Hopleys' This well-mannered plant is, unfortunately, slow to multiply. It produces flat sprays of soft lilac flowers that lighten in colour as they age. 75 cm (2½ft).

'Lambrook Mauve' A delightful, low clump-forming plant with soft mauve-pink flowers. AGM. Late spring to early summer. 60 cm (2 ft).

pauciflorum Unlike the others, this produces sprays of long, tubular, lemon flowers, each tinted with bronzy red. It forms a dense mound with a mass of rather furry stems. Summer. 60 cm (2 ft).

Polemonium caeruleum

Polemonium carneum

Polemonium 'Hopleys'

Polemonium 'Lambrook Mauve'

Polemonium pauciflorum

POLYGONATUM *x hybridum*
(Solomon's Seal)

An elegant, gently spreading plant. It produces small, green-tinged, cream bells that dangle in pairs along arching stems, to give themselves maximum exposure. The leaves are mid-green and oval. Grow in a fertile, well-drained soil that remains moist, in light shade. A north-facing border or woodland site is ideal. Early to late spring. AGM. 105 cm (3½ft).

POLYSTICHUM *setiferum* 'Acutilobum'
(Shield Fern)

An extremely handsome fern with prostrate, triangular leaves. Each frond is further divided into lacy leaflets, rich green in colour and bronze as they uncurl in spring. A deciduous plant for moist shade. 60 cm (2 ft).

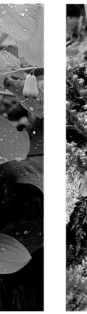

Polygonatum x hybridum

Polystichum setiferum 'Acutilobum'

Potentilla atrosanguinea

POTENTILLA (Cinquefoil)

These cheerful plants are prolific in their quantity of flower production. Small, strawberry-like blooms are carried in sprays above leafy growth that is either spreading and relaxed, or upright and clump-forming. The low varieties are useful for edging borders, while the taller types slot nicely into mixed planting schemes with other perennials. Grow in any well-drained soil, in sun or partial shade.

atrosanguinea An attractive combination of red and silver. Arching stems produce single, truly scarlet flowers above a neat clump of leaves. Above, these are rendered silver with soft, silvery hairs; beneath, they are almost entirely white. Early summer. 30 cm (1 ft).

'Etna' Very dark maroon, single flowers are carried on a network of relaxed stems that form a broad mound with mid-green leaves. Midsummer. 45 cm (18 in).

'Gibson's Scarlet' A mass of single, vivid red flowers with black centres is borne on long, lax stems. Its leaves are mid-green. AGM. Summer. 45 cm (18 in).

x hopwoodiana A charming plant with soft salmon-pink flowers, each flushed with scarlet. These are carried on long, arching stems above mid-green foliage. Summer. 45 cm (18 in).

Potentilla 'Etna'

Potentilla 'Gibson's Scarlet'

Potentilla x hopwoodiana

Potentilla nepalensis 'Roxana'

Potentilla recta sulphurea

Potentilla recta 'Warrenii'

nepalensis 'Roxana' A spreading variety with single, vermilion flowers, maroon centres and red stems. Summer. 45 cm (18 in).

recta sulphurea Large, soft lemon flowers that are carried in clusters on erect, leafy stems with light green foliage. AGM. Summer. 60 cm (2 ft).

recta 'Warrenii' Bright cadmium-yellow flowers, emerging from hairy buds, are carried on an erect plant with mid-green, tooth-edged leaves. Summer. 60 cm (2 ft).

rupestris A variety that flowers profusely. Pure white, yellow-centred, cupped flowers are produced in ample sprays on much branched, slender stems above a clump of dark green foliage. Late spring. 60 cm (2 ft).

'William Rollison' Ruffled, semi-double, vermilion flowers, with highlights of yellow, are borne on long, lax stems. AGM. Summer. 45 cm (18 in).

'Yellow Queen' A bright yellow variety with semi-double flowers, like prize rosettes, held on long stems. 45 cm (18 in).

Potentilla rupestris

Potentilla 'William Rollison'

Potentilla 'Yellow Queen'

Primula chionantha

Primula denticulata

Primula japonica 'Miller's Crimson'

PRIMULA

In its wild form, this large and diverse family can be found throughout the Northern Hemisphere. As border plants they are both charming and colourful, providing spots of colour for small areas or drifts of colour in large planting schemes. Suitable for growing along the edge of ponds, moist woodlands and damp borders, primulas can be divided into two groups. One group contains low-growing varieties that present their flowers just above the leaves. The other produces clusters of flowers at the top of erect stems. All possess a basal clump of long leaves and require a soil that retains its moisture. Some varieties need a boggy soil, but all will survive in shade.

'Candelabra' varieties These are upright plants suitable for growing in large groups. They produce whorls of small flowers on stems that tend to be felted with white. The blooms are single, trumpet-shaped and found in shades of violet, pale ruby-red or soft orange. If individual colours are required, they can be purchased by variety under the following names: *Primula beesiana* (rich pink); *P. bulleyana* (orange); *P. cockburniana* (red-orange). However, when planted together they will seed themselves into a most wonderful array of colours. Grow along the edges of boggy areas, still ponds and quiet streams. Midsummer. 60 cm (2 ft).

chionantha This delightful little plant has pendant-like, highly fragrant, white flowers, with a violet eye. These are produced on long, woolly stems above a rosette of long, thin, pale green leaves. AGM. Spring. 45 cm (18 in).

denticulata (Drumstick Primula) A curious little plant that forms a tight ball with small flowers of lilac, mauve or white. These are balanced, like drumsticks, on tall stems above mid-green leaves. AGM. Spring. 30 cm (1 ft).

florindae (Giant Cowslip) The common name of this plant refers to its soft yellow flowers. These are highly fragrant and borne in dangling clusters on upright stems. A variety for boggy soils. AGM. Midsummer. 60 cm (2 ft).

japonica **'Miller's Crimson'** Whorls of crimson flowers are carried on grey felted stems above mid-green leaves. An ideal plant for growing along streams and ponds in light shade. Late spring. 60 cm (2 ft).

japonica **'Postford White'** Pure white flowers, each with a yellow eye, are carried in whorls on tall, erect stems. Its leaves are toothed and light green. It needs to be grown in boggy places. Early summer. 60 cm (2 ft).

Primula florindae

Primula japonica 'Postford White'

Primula pulverulenta

Primula veris hybrids

pulverulenta Another variety for damp spots, with tiers of wine-red blooms, carried in whorls, on grey stems. AGM. Early summer. 60 cm (2 ft).

veris **hybrids** (Cowslip) The European cowslip, found in grassy areas and light woodland, is one of the prettiest wild flowers. Its cultivated form, although charming, is generally grown from seed and is therefore variable in flower colour. However, these are always yellow, trumpet-shaped, fragrant and held in clusters on erect stems. Early summer. 30 cm (1 ft).

vulgaris (Primrose) The primrose is a European native found, like *P. veris*, in grassy areas and woodland. It has flat, pale lemon flowers which, like *P. veris* in its cultivated form, produce a mixed batch of colour tones. The flowers are held in clusters and nestle within a rosette of mid-green leaves. Spring. 15 cm (6 in).

vulgaris double hybrids

During the 19th century the primrose became a plant of great value to cottage gardeners. Seedlings were selected by enthusiasts, which led to the introduction of these double-flowered forms. Having been neglected for many years, they were reintroduced into commercial horticulture during the 1980s. The flowers form neat, double rosettes and are held in dense clusters within its mid-green leaves. Spring.

'Dawn Ansell' Creamy white flowers. 15 cm (6 in).

'Marie Crousse' Mauve-pink flowers edged with white. 15 cm (6 in).

Primula vulgaris

Primula 'Marie Crousse'

Primula 'Dawn Ansell'

Primula 'Miss Indigo'

'**Miss Indigo**' Deep violet flowers with white edging. 15 cm (6 in).

'**Sue Jervis**' Apricot flowers which, on further inspection, are lemon yellow with an overlay of dusky pink. 15 cm (6 in).

'**Sunshine Susie**' Golden yellow flowers. 15 cm (6 in).

vulgaris '**Lilacina Plena**' Softest lilac flowers. It is lovely planted with pulmonarias and is also listed as *P*. 'Quaker's Bonnet'. 15 cm (6 in).

Primula 'Sue Jervis'

Primula 'Sunshine Susie'   Primula vulgaris 'Lilacina Plena'

Prunella grandiflora 'Alba'

Prunella grandiflora 'Loveliness'

Pulmonaria angustifolia azurea

Pulmonaria angustifolia 'Blaues Meer'

Pulmonaria 'Blue Ensign'

Pulmonaria 'Lewis Palmer'

PRUNELLA (Seal Heal)

A very useful carpeting plant with large, hooded flowers borne in short, dumpy spikes above deep green leaves. Like many ground-cover plants, it can become invasive, so make sure its partners are robust. Easy to grow in any well-drained soil, in sun or partial shade. Early to midsummer.

grandiflora **'Alba'** White flowers. 15 cm (6in).

grandiflora **'Loveliness'** Lilac flowers. AGM. 15 cm (6 in).

PULMONARIA
(Lungwort)

Almost the first of spring's delights, bringing with it the promise of warmer weather and lighter nights. These low-growing plants bear clusters, or sprays, of trumpet-like flowers for weeks on end above mounds of decorative, long, mid-green leaves. Often these are marked with silver spots, which accounts for its common name. They are ideal for planting beneath deciduous shrubs or in lightly shaded areas and like a soil that does not dry out during the summer. Spring.

angustifolia azurea Flat sprays of brilliant blue flowers emerge from mauve buds above a low, spreading clump of smooth, mid-green leaves. 23 cm (9 in).

angustifolia **'Blaues Meer'** Clusters of purple buds burst into small, vivid blue flowers. The leaves are smooth and deep green. 25 cm (10 in).

'Blue Ensign' A spreading plant with violet-blue flowers appearing from purple buds and deep green, pointed leaves. 30 cm (1 ft).

'Lewis Palmer' This, in my opinion, is the best rich blue-flowered variety. An upright plant produces clusters of flowers above a mound of spotted leaves. It flowers for a long time and is excellent with *Valeriana phu aurea* and *Centaurea montana*. AGM. 45 cm (18 in).

Pulmonaria longifolia

longifolia Graceful, arching stems are topped with tight clusters of funnel-shaped, vivid blue flowers. It produces a decorative low clump of long, slim leaves that are evenly spotted and splashed with white. 23 cm (9 in).

'Margery Fish' A handsome plant. Wide, violet-blue flowers are borne on arched stems above a spreading clump of wrinkle-edged, almost silver leaves. AGM. 30 cm (1 ft).

officinalis **'Sissinghurst White'** The best white-flowered variety. A vigorous and domed clump of silver-marked, pale green leaves produces small sprays of delicate, pure white flowers. AGM. 25 cm (10 in).

'Roy Davidson' Open sprays of little, soft blue flowers are borne above a low-growing mound of evenly spotted leaves. 25 cm (10 in).

'Opal' An excellent variety with tight clusters of pale sky-blue flowers, opening from palest pink buds. Its foliage forms a low, neatly spreading clump with oval, leopard spotted leaves. Lovely with *Stachys byzantina* and other silver foliaged plants. 30 cm (1 ft).

rubra A variety which has many similar sisters. Loose clusters of open, coral-red flowers are carried in profusion above evergreen, soft green leaves, gently wrinkled at the edges. Similar varieties are: *P. rubra* 'Redstart', which is more robust, but the flowers are smaller; and *P. rubra* 'Bowles Red', which flowers a little later. AGM. 30 cm (1 ft).

Pulmonaria 'Margery Fish'

Pulmonaria 'Roy Davidson'

Pulmonaria officinalis 'Sissinghurst White'

Pulmonaria 'Opal'

Pulmonaria rubra

Pulmonaria rubra 'David Ward'

Pulmonaria rubra 'Barfield Pink'

rubra 'Barfield Pink' This produces relaxed stems of pink flowers, not dissimilar to *P. rubra*, but each flower is a paler pink around the edges. The foliage is gently spotted with white. 30 cm (1 ft).

rubra 'David Ward' A handsome plant for brightening up a shady corner. A flat rosette of white-edged, pale green leaves gives rise to broad clusters of coral-red flowers. 23 cm (9 in).

saccharata 'Argentea' A useful plant for its foliage, which is just about silver. The sprays of small, violet-blue flowers are not over-exciting, but the whole plant has an airy feel. AGM. 30 cm (1 ft).

saccharata 'Dora Bielefeld' Soft green foliage, freckled with white spots, produces open clusters of soft pink flowers to form a gentle, rounded plant. 23 cm (9 in).

saccharata 'Frühlingshimmel' A pretty plant with airy sprays of pale blue flowers. These emerge from pink buds above a clump of small, gently spotted leaves. 30 cm (1 ft).

saccharata 'Mrs. Moon' Soft blue flowers, opening from coral-pink buds, smother a perfectly domed clump of small, lightly spotted, round leaves. 30 cm (1 ft).

Pulmonaria saccharata 'Dora Bielefeld'

Pulmonaria saccharata 'Argentea'

Pulmonaria saccharata 'Frühlingshimmel'

Pulmonaria saccharata 'Mrs. Moon'

Ranunculus aconitifolius 'Flore Pleno'

RANUNCULUS (Buttercup)

I have a soft spot for these small, mainly bright yellow plants. They remind me of the British countryside in early summer, when roadside verges are full of the rich yellow mist of buttercups and the white of cow parsley. They are easy to grow requiring a soil that remains moist, in sun or partial shade. Late spring into early summer.

aconitifolius **'Flore Pleno'** (White Bachelor's Buttons) Perfectly shaped little white pompons are produced on branched, red stems. At its base and at each branch, large, deeply divided, soft green foliage is produced. AGM. 75 cm (2½ft).

acris citrinus A delicate plant with cupped soft yellow flowers, that are slightly lighter in the middle. These are borne in sprays on branched stems with mid-green leaves. 60 cm (2 ft).

acris **'Flore Pleno'** (Bachelor's Buttons) An airy haze of yellow is created by sprays of small, double, golden yellow buttons. The flowers are borne on long, wiry stems above a low clump of deeply split, mid-green foliage. I grow this amongst hostas. 60 cm (2 ft).

constantinopolitanus **'Plenus'** A mouthful, or what? Large, very double flowers of yellow form a neat mound with deeply cut leaves. This is a spreading plant that needs a very moist soil. 30 cm (1 ft).

gramineus A small plant for the front of a border. It produces clusters of glossy, brilliant yellow buttercups on upright, well-branched stems. At its base is a dense tuft of grassy, grey-green leaves. AGM. 30 cm (1 ft).

Ranunculus acris citrinus

Ranunculus acris 'Flore Pleno'

Ranunculus constantinopolitanus 'Plenus'

Ranunculus gramineus

RHEUM (Chinese Rhubarb)

These members of the rhubarb family produce highly ornamental leaves. They are large, ragged at the edges and form immense clumps that need both space and moisture to be at their best. Eventually, thick stems erupt from bulbous mounds and bear upright spikes of tiny, beadlike flowers. They will grow in any moisture-retentive soil, in sun or partial shade. Summer.

palmatum Large, rich red leaves burst from a hefty central crown. Later, they become deep green, but still remain red underneath. Later still, stout stems produce plumes of fluffy, cream flowers. AGM. 180 cm (6 ft).

palmatum 'Atrosanguineum' A very handsome plant with immense dark green leaves. These are red underneath, the texture of chamois leather and cut into jagged points around the edges. Later, large buds, like fists, push themselves through the soil to produce tiny flowers of rich red-pink. 180 cm (6 ft).

RHODIOLA *rosea* (Roseroot)

Once listed as *Sedum rhodiola*, this is to me still more like a *Sedum* than anything else. A plant of rocky areas, it grows into perfectly domed mounds with short stems bearing round, grey leaves. Each stem is topped with a rounded cluster of tiny, lime-green flowers. Grow in a well-drained or dry soil, in sun. Summer. 30 cm (1 ft).

RODGERSIA

A plant for damp situations. It produces handsome leaves that should belong to a large tree rather than a herbaceous plant. These are round and further segmented into three or five leaflets. They form slowly spreading clumps and send up tall, arching stems topped with clusters of small flowers. Grow in any soil that remains moist or damp, in sun or dappled shade. Summer.

henrici Tiny, papery, buff-pink flowers are held in bunches at the end of each branched stem, like an elegant tree. Its leaves are broad, deep green and roughly textured. 90 cm (3 ft).

pinnata Very large leaves, bumpy-textured and hairy underneath, produce starlike flowers in shades of white, red or pink. These are borne in tiers on red, whiskered stems. 120 cm (4 ft).

Rheum palmatum

Rheum palmatum 'Atrosanguineum'

Rhodiola rosea

Rodgersia henrici

Rodgersia pinnata

podophylla A plant with handsome foliage. Each large leaf consists of five sections that are toothed around the edges and bronze when young. These grow into a dense clump and produce erect, branched stems that carry little domed clusters of tiny, cream flowers. AGM. 90 cm (3 ft).

sambucifolia Pyramids of fluffy white flowers are borne on pink-red stems above a creeping clump of mid-green leaves. These are thick and rough, looking like the leaves of the horse chestnut tree. 90 cm (3 ft).

ROMNEYA *coulteri*
(Californian Poppy, Tree Poppy)

I grow this choice subshrub as a perennial. It produces large, single white flowers with ruffled, tissue-thin petals that open out to reveal a boss of fine yellow stamens. These are borne singularly on erect, grey, well-branched stems with serrated, grey-green leaves. Although it can be difficult to grow, it will sucker freely once established and can become a nuisance. Therefore it is really only suitable for larger gardens. Grow in a very well-drained soil, sheltered away from cold winds, in the sun. AGM. Summer. 120 cm (4 ft).

ROSCOEA *purpurea*

An unusual plant with a long procession of purple flowers that are shaped like a helmeted man with a long, twinned beard. These are borne on upright stems above tall, mid-green, tulip-like leaves. It is a tuberous plant, found naturally in forests and meadows of the Himalayas, so grow it in a moist place, in partial shade. Midsummer. 45 cm (18 in).

Rodgersia podophylla

Rodgersia sambucifolia

Romneya coulteri

Roscoea purpurea

Rudbeckia fulgida deamii

RUDBECKIA (Black-Eyed Susan)

A cheerful, easily grown plant from North America for adding bright colour to borders. Daisy-shaped flowers with prominent centres are carried on erect, leafy stems to create a thick, spreading clump. Its leaves are heart-shaped and dark green. Grow in any soil that remains moist throughout the summer, in sun or partial shade. Late summer into early autumn.

fulgida deamii Handsome, large, bright golden yellow flowers, each with black centres. AGM. 60 cm (2 ft).

fulgida **'Goldsturm'** More abundant in flower than *R. fulgida deamii*. This produces large, golden yellow, star-shaped flowers with dark brown centres on strong, upright stems. AGM. 75 cm (2½ft).

'Herbstsonne' A monster of a plant, useful for the back of a border. Very tall stems produce, towards the top, large golden flowers with relaxed petals and a very green, domed centre. 180 cm (6 ft).

subtomentosa During my travels photographing plants, I occasionally came across a plant that I hadn't seen before, and this was one. It is rather more gentle than other rudbeckias, with very upright, slender stems, grooved and downy, and topped with a cluster of medium-sized, pure yellow flowers. 150 cm (5 ft).

Rudbeckia fulgida 'Goldsturm'

Rudbeckia subtomentosa

Rudbeckia 'Herbstsonne'

Salvia argentea

Salvia glutinosa

Salvia nemorosa 'Amethyst'

Salvia nemorosa 'Ostfriesland'

SALVIA
(Sage)

The sage family is a large one, containing not only perennials, but many half-hardy and short lived types. I have included mainly hardy forms, although the less hardy ones described will survive even in the cold of middle England. It is a diverse group, in botanical terms, with some varieties producing foliage in mounds, while others grow into open, upright plants. All bear mintlike flowers with two large, lower lips and, unless otherwise stated, mid-green leaves like those of sage. They are useful, if not to say essential, for knitting together groups of bolder plants and produce their flowers over a long period. Most varieties grow in any well-drained soil, in sun.

argentea I grow this plant for its rosette of large, ground-hugging leaves. These are spoon-shaped and coated thickly with a woolly covering of silver hairs. From these, tall, very branched stems emerge bearing large, translucent, white flowers. It is a short-lived perennial. AGM. Summer. 90 cm (3 ft).

glutinosa (Jupiter's Distaff) A very yellow plant with large, straw-yellow flowers. Each is striped inside with red and borne on long, sticky stems above large, yellow-green, heart-shaped leaves. Late summer into autumn. 105 cm (3½ft).

Salvia sclarea

nemorosa **'Amethyst'** A round, bushy plant with dense spikes of tiny, amethyst-blue flowers. AGM. Early to midsummer. 60 cm (2 ft).

nemorosa **'Lubecca'** A long-flowering variety with spikes of small, rich blue flowers. Early to midsummer. AGM. 45 cm (18 in).

nemorosa **'Ostfriesland'** A little bigger and later than S. x *sylvestris* 'Mainacht', but otherwise with the same rich blue flowers. AGM. Early to midsummer. 60 cm (2 ft).

sclarea (Clary) A short-lived perennial that happily seeds itself around. It produces very branched stems thickly set with white and pink, large lipped flowers. The leaves are large and deep green. Grow in a well-drained soil, including a poor gravelly one, in sun. Summer. 75 cm (2½ft).

x superba Upright violet-blue flower spikes are produced above a round, bushy plant. AGM. Summer. 60 cm (2 ft).

Salvia nemorosa 'Lubecca'

Salvia x superba

Salvia x sylvestris 'Blauhügel'

Salvia x sylvestris 'Schneehügel'

Salvia uliginosa

x sylvestris **'Blauhügel'** Slender spikes of soft lavender-blue flowers above a mound of mid-green foliage. AGM. Summer. 60 cm (2 ft).

x sylvestris **'Mainacht'** A long-flowering variety with spikes of tiny, deep blue flowers borne above a round clump of leaves. AGM. Summer. 60 cm (2 ft).

x sylvestris **'Schneehügel'** White flowers in dense spikes are carried above a mound of light green leaves. Summer. 45 cm (18 in).

transsylvanica A plant that resembles a *Nepeta* rather than a *Salvia*. Long sticky stems with dark green leaves carry indigo blue flowers. It is ideal for the middle of the border. Summer. 105 cm (3½ft).

uliginosa A late-flowering plant for the back of a border. Long stems, lightly clothed with both flowers and foliage form an elegant, open clump. The flowers are sky blue and, when planted with tall asters, perfect for an autumn border. It needs a warm site with moist soil. AGM. Autumn. 180 cm (6 ft).

verticillata A loose clump is made up of soft, leafy stems that end in short spikes of soft lilac-blue flowers. These arch gently at the top and are loved by bees and butterflies. It is a gentle plant suitable for borders of mixed perennials. Midsummer into autumn. 60 cm (2 ft).

verticillata **'Alba'** Spikes of small, pure white flowers emerge from soft green calyces on long stems with soft green foliage. Midsummer into autumn. 60 cm (2 ft).

verticillata **'Purple Rain'** A richly coloured plant with spikes of purple flowers produced for a long period on leafy stems. It is lovely with yellow roses. Midsummer into autumn. 60 cm (2 ft).

Salvia x sylvestris 'Mainacht'

Salvia transsylvanica

Salvia verticillata

Salvia verticillata 'Alba'

Salvia verticillata 'Purple Rain'

Sanguisorba albiflora

Sanguisorba canadensis

Sanguisorba tenuifolia

SANGUISORBA (Burnet)

Not all border plants can be extroverts. Indeed, if they were, we would soon tire of them. These are subtle and have long, slender stems bearing poker-like spikes of tiny flowers. At the base, they produce a clump of deeply divided, mid-green foliage. All require a well-drained soil that does not dry out, in sun or partial shade.

albiflora Rather odd white flowers that look like long pink pigs wearing shaggy, long-haired white coats. These dip gently at the end of long, branched stems. Midsummer. 90 cm (3 ft).

canadensis (Canadian Burnet) A tall, upright plant with tight, fluffy spikes of tiny, cream flowers. 150 cm (5 ft).

obtusa A plant with long, fluffy, bottle-brush shaped, pink flowers that dangle from slender stems. Midsummer. 90 cm (3 ft).

tenuifolia Small, tight pokers of dusky maroon flowers that are held horizontally to its upright, slender stems. At the base sit mid-green leaves that are neatly 'pinked' around the edges. Autumn. 120 cm (4 ft).

Sanguisorba obtusa

SAPONARIA (Soapwort, Bouncing Bet)

Once grown as a detergent for washing clothes, it can still be found on roadside verges around the British countryside, marking the places where villages once stood. It has waxy, mid-green leaves that exude a soapy froth when rubbed between the fingers. These are borne on brittle stems with large clusters of simple, phloxlike flowers. A robust plant, this will grow in any well-drained soil, in sun or partial shade. Summer.

officinalis Softest pink flowers are produced from swollen, bladder-like calyces. 90 cm (3 ft).

officinalis '**Rosea Plena**' A double form of *Saponaria officinalis* with pale pink flowers. 90 cm (3 ft).

Saponaria officinalis

Saponaria officinalis 'Rosea Plena'

Saxifraga x urbium

Scabiosa caucasica 'Miss Willmott'

Scabiosa columbaria 'Butterfly Blue'

Scabiosa columbaria 'Pink Mist'

SAXIFRAGA *x urbium* (London Pride)

Not so long ago, this tough plant was readily found edging paths and borders. But like so many once 'common' plants, it is now grown less often. A vigorous, weed excluding carpet is made up of spoonlike, rich green, leathery leaves. These are scalloped around the edges and bear slender stems of small, white flowers, gently tinged with pink. Grow in any soil, including poor ones, in sun or partial shade. AGM. Summer. 30 cm (1 ft).

SCABIOSA
(Scabious, Pink Cushion Flower)

Delightfully elegant plants that produce a long succession of disc-shaped flowers throughout the summer. These are found in gentle colours and spring from a basal clump of long, serrated, mid-green leaves. They are excellent for cutting, as well as planting at the front of a border. Being plants of meadows and rocky situations, they will grow in any very well-drained soil, that is not too rich, in sun. Summer.

caucasica **'Clive Greaves'** Large, soft lavender-blue flowers with a white centre. AGM. 45 cm (18 in).

caucasica **'Miss Willmott'** Creamy white flowers. AGM. 45 cm (18 in).

'Chile Black' An interesting, recently introduced plant. It produces an upright clump with leafy, branched stems that are topped with round flowers of deepest maroon. These, at a distance, are almost black and bloom for weeks on end. 75 cm (2½ft).

columbaria **'Butterfly Blue'** A newer hybrid from the mid-1980s that was launched with great gusto. It produces large quantities of neat, soft blue flowers above a dome of leaves. 30 cm (1 ft).

columbaria *ochroleuca* Delicate, small, lemon blooms are carried on long, very slender stems. 45 cm (18 in).

columbaria **'Pink Mist'** A pretty counterpart to *S. columbaria* 'Butterfly Blue' with lavender-pink flowers. 30 cm (1 ft).

lucida A mound of finely divided, mid-green foliage abundantly sprouts slender stems of small, lilac flowers. 45 cm (18 in).

Scabiosa caucasica 'Clive Greaves'

Scabiosa 'Chile Black'

Scabiosa columbaria ochroleuca

Scabiosa lucida

Schizostylis coccinea

Schizostylis coccinea 'Major'

Schizostylis coccinea 'Mrs. Hegarty'

SCHIZOSTYLIS (Kaffir Lily)

Most autumn-flowering plants produce daisy-like blooms. These are quite different and have clusters of cupped, starry flowers elegantly emerging from slender, soft green stems. Each flower has four broad, silky petals and is borne above soft green, grassy leaves to form a slowly spreading clump. They are an absolute must for a sheltered spot. Grow in any well-drained soil, in sun or partial shade. Mid to late autumn.

coccinea Deep red-pink flowers. 60 cm (2 ft).

coccinea alba Pure white flowers. 60 cm (2 ft).

coccinea **'Major'** Large, deep pink-red flowers. AGM. 60 cm (2 ft).

coccinea **'Mrs. Hegarty'** Soft pink flowers. 60 cm (2 ft).

coccinea **'Sunrise'** Coral-pink flowers. 60 cm (2 ft).

SCROPHULARIA *auriculata* **'Variegata'** (Water Figwort)

A tall, upright plant for moist or wet soils. It produces lots of crinkled grey-green leaves, unevenly edged with cream, on square slender stems. These carry tiny, maroon, funnel-shaped flowers. It is useful for brightening the back of a border or the edge of ponds. Plant in sun or partial shade. Summer. 120 cm (4 ft).

Schizostylis coccinea alba

Scrophularia auriculata 'Variegata'

Schizostylis coccinea 'Sunrise'

Sedum 'Bertram Anderson'

Sedum 'Herbstfreude'

Sedum 'Ruby Glow'

Sedum spectabile

Sedum 'Frosty Morn'

SEDUM (Ice Plant)

These need very little attention to succeed and are among the easiest plants to grow. They form well-behaved clumps, or spreading mounds, with thick, succulent leaves that look attractive throughout the growing season. In late summer, clusters of buds burst into tiny, starry flowers and last well into the autumn. They are an essential food for bees and butterflies, blooming at a time when these creatures are preparing to take a long winter sleep. Plant in any well-drained soil, including dry ones, in sun. Late summer into autumn.

'**Bertram Anderson**' A prostrate plant with purplish foliage and arching stems ending in open clusters of rich red flowers. AGM. 23 cm (9 in).

'**Frosty Morn**' An upright plant with oval, pale green leaves, irregularly edged with cream. Later, these are topped with conical heads of pale pink flowers. 60 cm (2 ft).

'**Herbstfreude**' A sturdy clump of thick stems bears heavy, flat heads of rich rose-pink flowers. These deepen to wine-red and last for weeks above fleshy, pale green leaves. It is a particularly good butterfly plant. AGM. 60 cm (2 ft).

'**Ruby Glow**' Clusters of rich red flowers, like rubies, are borne in loose clusters on prostrate stems with purple-grey foliage. This is ideal for edging a border and particularly effective with grey plants such as *Stachys byzantina*. AGM. 23 cm (9 in).

spectabile I grow this with rich blue asters, as they combine perfectly with its pale pink flowers. These are carried in broad, flat heads on sturdy, upright stems to form a round mound with pale green, fleshy leaves. AGM. 45 cm (18 in).

Sedum spectabile 'Iceberg'

Sedum telephium maximum 'Atropurpurea'

spectabile **'Iceberg'** Tiny, crystal-white flowers are borne in wide heads with palest green foliage. It sometimes produces flowers of soft pink, but consider these a happy accident. 45 cm (18 in).

telephium maximum **'Atropurpurea'** Rich red-brown stems are branched and carry small sprays of rich pink flowers. It creates an open, spreading plant. 45 cm (18 in).

telephium **'Matrona'** An very attractive variety. It produces wide, but not too large, heads of small, soft rose-pink flowers with pale pink sepals. These are carried on upright stems with rich green leaves. 45 cm (18 in).

telephium **'Munstead Red'** A handsome, rather dusky, upright plant with dark red flowers held in broad clusters above purple-green stems and leaves. 60 cm (2 ft).

SENECIO *doria*

This rather coarse plant is excellent for using at the back of a large border. It produces an erect, leafy clump with large, bright green leaves. These are topped with loose, broad heads of small, daisy-shaped, bright yellow flowers. Grow in any well-drained soil, rich or poor, in sun or partial shade. Midsummer. 180 cm (6 ft).

Sedum telephium 'Matrona'

Sedum telephium 'Munstead Red'

Senecio doria

SIDALCEA (False Mallow, Checkerbloom, Prairie Mallow)

These gentle plants have tall, straight stems bearing lots of open, paper-thin blooms, which resemble the flowers of a hollyhock. At the base, mid-green, deeply divided leaves form a good mound. They are ideal for the middle of a mixed border, but to maintain their vigour they should be divided every three years. Grow in sun, in any soil that does not dry out. Midsummer.

candida Pure white flowers. 60 cm (2 ft).

'Elsie Heugh' Very pale pink flowers, delicately fringed around the edges. 90 cm (3 ft).

'Rose Queen' Deep rose-pink flowers. 90 cm (3 ft).

'Sussex Beauty' Soft pink flowers, deeper than those of *Sidalcea* 'Elsie Heugh'. 90 cm (3 ft).

SISYRINCHIUM

A useful clump-forming, long-flowering plant with evergreen, swordlike leaves, rather like those of an iris. From these arise stiff, erect stems studded with small, single flowers. Unfortunately, it can be short-lived, but if allowed it will seed itself around. Grow in any very well-drained soil, in sun. Midsummer.

striatum Pale yellow flowers and grey-green leaves. 75 cm (2½ ft).

striatum **'Aunt May'** A variegated form of *S. striatum* with cream striped foliage. It is not as vigorous as the green version, but has the same cream flowers. 60 cm (2 ft).

Sidalcea candida

Sidalcea 'Elsie Heugh'

Sidalcea 'Rose Queen'

Sidalcea 'Sussex Beauty'

Sisyrinchium striatum

Sisyrinchium striatum 'Aunt May'

Smilacina racemosa

SMILACINA *racemosa*
(False Solomon's Seal)

This is a slowly spreading, clump-forming
plant. It produces leafy, upright stems
that end in short, feathery spikes of tiny,
heavily scented, white flowers. The leaves
are oval and pleated. Grow in a shady
spot that is not too dry, such as a lightly
wooded area. Late spring. 90 cm (3 ft).

SMYRNIUM *perfoliatum*
(Perfoliate Alexanders)

A curiosity for a shady spot, with round
leaves of light green that work their way
up a rigid stem. These end in loose
umbels of small, lime-coloured flowers.
The whole plant reminds me of a
Euphorbia. However, it is a biennial, so
allow it to seed around. Plant in well-
drained soil that remains moist, in sun
or shade. Spring. 60 cm (2 ft).

Smyrnium perfoliatum

SOLIDAGO (Golden Rod)

I struggle to like these plants. However,
they are useful for adding colour to a
border of late perennials. They produce
feathery sprays of tiny, golden yellow
flowers on leafy stems with linear, mid-
green foliage that grows into a
spreading clump. Plant in any well-
drained soil, in sun or partial shade.
Late summer into early autumn.

'Golden King' A low-growing variety with
spikes of golden flowers splaying out
horizontally to the stems. 45 cm (18 in).

'Loddon' A tall plant with broad,
tapering spires of golden yellow
flowers. 90 cm (3 ft).

Solidago 'Golden King'

Solidago 'Loddon'

STACHYS

Like salvias, this group of plants is diverse and extremely useful – no garden should be without at least one type. There are two different forms; one is the ubiquitous furry, silver-foliaged sort that is just about evergreen; the other grows into dense, upright clumps with dark green leaves. All produce flowers on erect, leafy stems and grow in a well-drained soil, that does not dry out during summer, in sun. Summer.

Stachys byzantina

Stachys byzantina 'Big Ears'

Stachys byzantina 'Silver Carpet'

byzantina (Lamb's Ears) A thick carpet of silver-grey, felted leaves, as soft as the ears of a rabbit, sends up woolly, grey stems, from which tiny, pink-mauve flowers sprout. This quickly spreading plant is useful for any size of border especially those with soft pink- or blue-flowered plants. 45 cm (18 in).

***byzantina* 'Big Ears'** I originally bought this plant as *Stachys byzantina*, then found it under this very appropriate name. Large mounds are formed from bold, smoothly shaped, silver-grey leaves. The flower stems, which are not abundant, tend to be lax. It is a plant with architectural appeal, ideal for larger borders. 60 cm (2 ft).

***byzantina* 'Primrose Heron'** A plant that I like to place among other yellow varieties and which is, happily, not as vigorous as the silver forms. The furry leaves emerge as pale green, change to yellow-green, then transform to soft yellow. It produces the usual pink-mauve flowers. 45 cm (18 in).

***byzantina* 'Silver Carpet'** This is a non-flowering form of *Stachys byzantina* and an excellent plant for the front of a border. It is extremely vigorous, producing a dense carpet of soft, almost woolly, leaves that are more silver than grey. 15 cm (6 in).

***byzantina* 'Striped Phantom'** A bright addition to a border, although less commonly available. Its woolly, grey leaves are decorated with liberal splashes of cream and produce stems of pink-mauve flowers. Remove any plain grey shoots to maintain its variegation. 30 cm (1 ft).

Stachys byzantina 'Primrose Heron'

Stachys byzantina 'Striped Phantom'

Stachys cretica

cretica A non-spreading plant, which is the least hardy member of the silver-leaved section. Soft, silvery, slightly wrinkled leaves form evergreen hummocks. From this sprout square, ridged stems bearing, at neat intervals, clusters of small, pink flowers. It needs a warm, very well-drained, poor soil, in sun. 60 cm (2 ft).

macrantha 'Superba' An excellent border plant for mixing with other perennials. This produces a broad clump with large, mid-green leaves and dense, upright spikes of large, pink-purple flowers. 75 cm (2½ft).

officinalis 'Alba' (Wood Betony) A lovely combination of deep green and pure white. Short, fat spikes of small, pure white flowers are borne on upright stems above a mounding mat of deep green, scalloped-edged leaves. 45 cm (18 in).

officinalis 'Rosea Superba' A very erect plant. Upright, bright green stems are topped with tight spikes of small, pink flowers. These are thickly produced above a tidy clump of long, fresh green leaves. 60 cm (2 ft).

STIPA

I consider these to be the most handsome of ornamental grasses. They produce mounds of long, slender leaves and elegant spikes of flowers. Both varieties mentioned will grow in a well-drained soil, in sun. Midsummer.

calamagrostis A domed mound of long, blue-green foliage produces arching stems of feathery, golden brown flowers. 75 cm (2½ft).

gigantea (Giant Feather Grass) This is a magnificent grass. A trailing hummock of fine, arching leaves gives rise to tall, rigid stems that end in an eruption of oat-shaped flowers. These open further into cascading, feathery sprays that last for months. A plant for a special spot. AGM. 180 cm (6 ft).

Stachys macrantha 'Superba'

Stachys officinalis 'Alba'

Stachys officinalis 'Rosea Superba'

Stipa calamagrostis

Stipa gigantea

Stokesia laevis

Stokesia laevis 'Alba'

STOKESIA (Stokes' Aster)

These rather odd plants produce large flowers that are carried individually on straight, leafy stems. The blooms are stiffly cupped, with petals rather like those of a cornflower. At the base, long straplike, mid-green leaves form an evergreen rosette. They need a well-drained soil, a little on the acid side, that remains moist, in sun. Late summer into early autumn.

laevis Light blue flowers. 45 cm (18 in).

laevis **'Alba'** Creamy white flowers. 45 cm (18 in).

laevis **'Mary Gregory'** Primrose-yellow flowers with light green foliage. 45 cm (18 in).

STROBILANTHES *atropurpurea*

A gentle and unusual plant with sprays of violet-blue, funnel-shaped flowers. These are carried on long, branched stems with dark green, heart-shaped leaves. It forms an open, upright bush suitable for the middle of the border, but this is not the most hardy of herbaceous perennials. To thrive, it requires a well-drained soil, in sun or partial shade. Mid to late summer. 120 cm (4 ft).

SYMPHYANDRA *hofmannii* (Bellflower)

A plant that definitely resembles a *Campanula*. It produces a basal clump of hairy, mid-green leaves and erect, leafy stems that shelter lots of nodding, cream, bell-like flowers. A short-lived plant for a very well-drained soil, in sun. Late spring into summer. 45 cm (18 in).

Stokesia laevis 'Mary Gregory'

Symphyandra hofmannii

Strobilanthes atropurpurea

SYMPHYTUM (Comfrey)

I have a tender spot for these more-often-than-not rampant colonisers. They are easy on the eye and to grow. Clusters of small, tubular flowers unfurl on long, hairy stems above thick clumps of broad leaves. If they get out of hand, they can be controlled easily with a spade. Grow in any soil, in sun and shade, including under shrubs and in rough areas. Spring.

azureum An upright plant with pale blue flowers, deep pink in bud, and soft grey-green foliage. It mixes well with *Geranium phaeum*. 90 cm (3 ft).

'Goldsmith' An attractive plant with yellow-edged, mid-green leaves that form a low, spreading carpet. Above this, clusters of soft blue flowers are borne. It is not as vigorous as some varieties, so remove any plain green leaves that appear to maintain the two-toned effect. 25 cm (10 in).

'Hidcote Blue' Curling sprays of red buds open into sky-blue flowers. These pale later to white and are carried above a lush, but invasive, mound of mid-green leaves. It is ideal for large areas that need to be filled quickly. 45 cm (18 in).

'Hidcote Pink' This is like *Symphytum* 'Hidcote Blue', but it has white bells, tinged with pink. In the shade it will flowers earlier. 45 cm (18 in).

ibericum A low, broad carpet of small, oval, dark green leaves produces curling sprays of cream flowers, pink in bud. 30 cm (1 ft).

Symphytum azureum

Symphytum 'Goldsmith'

Symphytum 'Hidcote Blue'

Symphytum ibericum

Symphytum 'Hidcote Pink'

Symphytum ibericum 'All Gold'

Symphytum officinale ochroleucum

Symphytum 'Rubrum'

Symphytum x uplandicum 'Variegatum'

ibericum **'All Gold'** In spring, this produces startling green-yellow leaves that form an upright clump. As the stems of pale blue flowers appear, the foliage deepens to mid-green. 90 cm (3 ft).

officinale ochroleucum A clean plant that may be difficult to acquire. It produces soft green foliage that is not too rampant, and erect stems with pure white flowers. 90 cm (3 ft).

'Rubrum' A non-invasive plant with a handsome balance of dark red flowers and dark green leaves. This is the last *Symphytum* to bloom, with hairy leaves forming an open, gently creeping clump. 45 cm (18 in).

x uplandicum **'Variegatum'** This is upright in habit, with handsome leaves of sage-green, broadly edged with white. Later, lilac-pink flowers are carried on erect stems. AGM. 90 cm (3 ft).

Tanacetum coccineum 'Eileen May Robinson'

Tanacetum vulgare 'Isla Gold'

Tellima grandiflora 'Rubra'

Tanacetum parthenium 'Rowallane'

Tellima grandiflora 'Odorata'

TANACETUM

A group of plants that are diverse in form. The obvious link is the shape of their leaves, which is deeply cut and aromatic. All types have herbal qualities and flowers that are shaped like daisies. They are excellent for growing in small borders with a well-drained soil, in sun.

coccineum **'Eileen May Robinson'** (Pyrethrum) This produces single, soft pink flowers on long stems above a clump of lacy, mid-green leaves. Some 15 years or so ago, pyrethrums, as they were then known, were easy to buy. However, for some reason they are now difficult to find. I wonder why. They flower all summer and make excellent cut flowers, but they do need protection from rabbits. AGM. Summer. 60 cm (2 ft).

parthenium **'Rowallane'** (Feverfew) An upright, aromatic plant with a basal mound of deeply divided, almost lacy, pale green leaves. Branched stems are topped with clusters of small, white, pompon-like flowers. This is a decorative form of the herb used for curing headaches that can be grown in partial shade as well as sun. Midsummer to autumn. 45 cm (18 in).

vulgare **'Isla Gold'** (Tansy) A spreading plant with the most vivid yellow foliage I have come across. The leaves are deeply divided and remain yellow throughout the year. Much later it produces upright, branched stems that are topped with small, yellow buttons. Summer. 60 cm (2 ft).

TELLIMA (Fringe Cups)

In no way can these be called dramatic. However, for a shady spot they are the plants to go for. Similar to tiarellas and heucheras in form, they grow into low, evergreen mounds with vine-shaped leaves and produce tall, slender stems of small bells. These evergreen plants will grow in the sun as long as the soil remains moist, but they prefer shady spots. Late spring.

grandiflora **'Odorata'** This produces small, whitish, fringed flowers that become pink with age. If you care to examine the flowers, you will find they are sweetly scented. The leaves are mid-green. 45 cm (18 in).

grandiflora **'Rubra'** A valuable variety with mid-green leaves which, in winter, become richly tinted with deep brown-red. As spring arrives, it produces stems of small pink bells. 45 cm (18 in).

Thalictrum aquilegiifolium

Thalictrum aquilegiifolium album

Thalictrum aquilegiifolium 'Thundercloud'

Thalictrum delavayi

Thalictrum delavayi 'Hewitt's Double'

THALICTRUM (Meadow Rue)

These handsome and dignified plants are suitable for the back of a border and woodland situations. They all produce small flowers in clusters or sprays, on elegant, upright, branched stems above mounds of decorative, deeply divided foliage. Grow in any soil that remains moist throughout the year, in sun or partial shade. Midsummer.

aquilegiifolium A reliable plant with mid-green, fernlike leaves that form a dense mound. From this arise erect stems with fluffy, round clusters of lilac-pink flowers. 120 cm (4 ft).

aquilegiifolium album A nice variation of *T. aquilegiifolium* with spiky heads of creamy white flowers. These look like little balls of cotton wool. 120 cm (4 ft).

aquilegiifolium **'Thundercloud'** An open, airy plant with sprays of spidery, violet flowers. These are borne on black stems above glaucous, mid-green foliage. AGM. 105 cm (3½ft).

delavayi This is a most elegant variety. From its mid-green clump of foliage, it produces soft mauve stems that are topped with small mauve flowers, each rendered fluffy with long anthers. AGM. 120 cm (4 ft).

delavayi **'Hewitt's Double'** This is a graceful, *Gypsophila*-like plant. It produces a mist of very small, double, lilac blooms on grey stems above mounds of mid-green leaves. AGM. 120 cm (4 ft).

Thalictrum flavum glaucum

Thalictrum flavum 'Illuminator'

flavum glaucum A handsome plant with thick, shiny, pale grey-green foliage and very upright, much-branched stems topped with a cluster of tiny, citrus-yellow flowers. It is ideal for a border with yellow flowers. AGM. 180 cm (6 ft).

flavum 'Illuminator' This is an interesting variation of *T. flavum glaucum*. In spring, the stems and leaves emerge in a translucent mixture of soft mauve and soft yellow, which reminds me of blanched celery. Later, as the leaves uncurl, the whole plant becomes pale green, and like its sister, it produces yellow flowers. 180 cm (6 ft).

THERMOPSIS *lanceolata* (False Lupin)

A North American perennial with black, slightly woolly stems of muted green leaves. These end in spires of soft yellow, lupin-like flowers to form a gently spreading, open clump. It will grow in a light, well-drained soil, in sun or partial shade. Late spring. 90 cm (3 ft).

TIARELLA *cordifolia* (Foam Flower)

A mounding, ground-cover plant similar to tellimas and heucheras with triangular leaves. It sends up slender stems with conical spikes of small, fluffy, cream flowers. During autumn, the leaves turn an attractive collection of red shades. To grow well, it needs a humus-rich soil that remains moist, in partial shade. AGM. Spring. 30 cm (1 ft).

TRACHYSTEMON *orientalis*

A useful rampant plant that is really only suitable for large gardens. Before the foliage emerges short, erect, hairy stems are produced bearing clusters of small, bright blue flowers, like those of borage. These remain as the large, rough, deep green leaves grow to form a thick, weed-excluding mound. Being a thug, it will grow in any soil and situation, including dry shade. Spring. 60 cm (2 ft).

Trachystemon orientalis

Thermopsis lanceolata

Tiarella cordifolia

Tradescantia x andersoniana 'Blue and Gold'

TRADESCANTIA (Spiderwort)

These are valuable plants, if only because they flower all summer. A weed-excluding thicket of grassy leaves produces many stems that carry, individually or in pairs, simple, three-petalled flowers, each with a fluffy centre of stamens. They are inclined to look tatty later in the year as the leaves become mottled with spots. Therefore, cut back during midsummer to allow new, clean foliage to emerge. They are easy to grow in any soil that remains moist in sun. Summer.

x andersoniana **'Blue and Gold'** Often the colour combination of yellow foliage and blue flowers can be rather unsatisfactory. However, the rich blue flowers and gold-green leaves of this variety makes a handsome and satisfactory combination. 45 cm (18 in).

x andersoniana **'Blue Stone'** Indigo blue flowers. 45 cm (18 in).

x andersoniana **'Concorde Grape'** Soft purple flowers with grey-green foliage. 45 cm (18 in).

x andersoniana **'Innocence'** Small white flowers with very pale violet stamens. 45 cm (18 in).

x andersoniana **'J.C. Weguelin'** One of the best varieties for quality of bloom, producing great quantities of soft violet-blue flowers. AGM. 45 cm (18 in).

x andersoniana **'Osprey'** Large white flowers with fluffy blue stamens. AGM. 45 cm (18 in).

x andersoniana **'Purple Dome'** Pure purple flowers. 45 cm (18 in).

Tradescantia x andersoniana 'Blue Stone'

Tradescantia x andersoniana 'Innocence'

Tradescantia x andersoniana 'Concorde Grape'

Tradescantia x andersoniana 'J.C. Weguelin'

Tradescantia x andersoniana 'Osprey'

Tradescantia x andersoniana 'Purple Dome'

Tricyrtis formosana

Tricyrtis 'Tojen'

TRICYRTIS (Toad Lily)

These unusual plants have extraordinarily shaped flowers. They are small, cupped, starry and each has a central tower of stamens, balanced like the blades of a helicopter, above the flower. These are carried on branched stems with oval, pointed leaves to form a leafy clump that spreads slowly. They are easy to grow and ideal for shady areas that remain moist. Autumn.

formosana An upright plant with soft purple flowers. On closer inspection, these are white and thickly spotted with purple. The leaves are glossy and dark green. AGM. 90 cm (3 ft).

'Tojen' A sprawling clump of very large, shiny leaves and sprays of white flowers, shaded around the edges with purple. 45 cm (18 in).

'White Towers' A short, erect plant with pure white flowers and soft green foliage. 60 cm (2 ft).

TRILLIUM (Wood Lily)

These are handsome woodland plants. They produce exotic, three-petalled flowers that sit neatly in the centre of three broad leaves. Although slow to multiply, they will eventually form a broad clump that can remain undisturbed for years. Grow in a moist, cool, humus-rich soil, in a shady spot. Spring.

erectum Open, nodding flowers with silky, maroon petals and a centre of large stamens. These are borne on short stems above shiny, mid-green leaves. AGM. 45 cm (18 in).

Tricyrtis 'White Towers'

Trillium erectum

Trillium grandiflorum

Trillium sessile

Trollius x cultorum 'Lemon Queen'

grandiflorum (Wake Robin) Vaselike, open flowers with broad, white petals and long anthers are produced above round, mid-green leaves. AGM. 30 cm (1 ft).

luteum Three slim, upward-pointing, pale yellow petals, that are actually sepals, arise from the centre of the leaves. These in colour are mottled with light and dark green. AGM. 30 cm (1 ft).

sessile (Toad-shade) An intriguing plant. Funnel-like, stemless flowers of very dark maroon emerge from a platform of large leaves. These are patterned with a mixture of army camouflage colours: light green, dark green and khaki. 30 cm (1 ft).

TROLLIUS (Globe Flower)

A plant for damp or wet soils, with flowers that are at first globe-shaped and later open into deeply cupped flowers. These are borne on erect stems above a dense mound of deep green, glossy leaves. They are ideal for bog gardens and for planting around the edges of streams or pools, in sun or partial shade. Spring.

chinensis '**Golden Queen**' Severely globe-shaped at first, the golden yellow flowers open into cups with a crown-like centre of upright petaloids. AGM. 45 cm (18 in).

x cultorum '**Lemon Queen**' A variety with gentle, pale yellow flowers. 60 cm (2 ft).

UVULARIA *grandiflora*
(Bellort, Merry Bells)

A dainty North American plant of great charm for a shady bed or woodland area. Dangling, bell-like, soft lemon flowers, the petals gently twisting, are carried individually on slender, upright stems with slim, mid-green leaves. These form a slowly spreading clump and require a moist, humus-rich soil with shade. Early spring. AGM. 60 cm (2 ft).

Trillium luteum

Trollius chinensis 'Golden Queen'

Uvularia grandiflora

VALERIANA (Valerian)

These are not particularly startling in terms of flower, but they produce highly decorative foliage. The tiny flowers, borne in umbels, are highly scented and carried on upright stems. They will grow in any soil that does not dry out, in sun or partial shade. Early summer.

officinalis sambucifolia This is a tall, elegant plant for mixed borders of perennials. A mound of pinnate, mid-green leaves produces stems that are very erect and topped with tight clusters of small, pure white flowers. 120 cm (4 ft).

phu 'Aurea' Never dismiss the importance of foliage in a border. In spring, this is a glorious plant. It produces bright yellow leaves, deeply divided and highlighted with soft green. These form a gently spreading clump. As the season progresses the leaves gradually mellow to soft green and give rise to short stems topped with umbels of small, starry white flowers. I grow it with blue spring flowers, such as pulmonarias. 90 cm (3 ft).

Valeriana officinalis sambucifolia

Valeriana phu 'Aurea'

Veratrum viride

Veratrum nigrum

Veratrum album

VERATRUM

These are uncommon plants, perhaps because they are slow to multiply and highly toxic. However, they produce ornamental clumps of large, mid-green leaves that are beautifully sculpted with deep veins and pleats. From these arise erect, well-branched stems. Each branch is coated with small, starry, rather unexciting flowers. These are plants for moist soils, in shade, and fit admirably into a woodland situation. Mid to late summer.

album (False Helleborine, White Helleborine) This is the most flowery variety of *Veratrum* with starry, white, green centred blooms. Occasionally, the flowers are pure green. 180 cm (6 ft).

nigrum This produces tall, straight stems, whitened with soft hairs. These are topped with horizontal branches that carry amazingly disappointing small, plain brown flowers. AGM. 120 cm (4 ft).

viride (Indian Poke) A North American variety with stems of yellow-green flowers. 180 cm (6 ft).

Verbascum chaixii album

VERBASCUM (Mullein)

If you want tall, elegant spikes of flowers in a border, these are your men. They produce upright stems that end in spires of simple, single flowers that open throughout the summer above a flat rosette of leaves. In the wild, these very handsome plants, can be found in poor soils. However, they will grow anywhere that is not waterlogged, in sun or partial shade. Summer.

chaixii album A white-flowered plant that carries its blooms in dense, slender spikes. Each pure white flower has a centre of soft purple stamens. 90 cm (3 ft).

chaixii **'Cotswold Beauty'** This produces terracotta flowers with mauve stamens that are carried on branched stems above grey-green foliage. AGM. 120 cm (4 ft).

chaixii **'Cotswold Queen'** A handsome variety with deep yellow flowers, purple stamens and grey-green leaves. 120 cm (4 ft).

chaixii **'Gainsborough'** A gently coloured variety with large, soft yellow flowers. These have yellow centres and are borne on grey-green stems. AGM. 120 cm (4 ft).

chaixii **'Mont Blanc'** A delicate sort of plant with pure white flowers, yellow centres and soft green foliage. 90 cm (3 ft).

Verbascum chaixii 'Cotswold Queen'

Verbascum chaixii 'Cotswold Beauty'

Verbascum chaixii 'Gainsborough'

Verbascum chaixii 'Mont Blanc'

chaixii **'Pink Domino'** Soft pink flowers with orange stamens. This combines perfectly with *Papaver orientale* 'Patty's Plum' and *Phlox paniculata* 'Norah Leigh'. AGM. 90 cm (3 ft).

'Helen Johnson' An attractive combination of caramel-coloured flowers, mauve stamens and grey felted leaves. Once a much sought-after plant, this is now becoming more available as other brown varieties are introduced. AGM. 90 cm (3 ft).

nigrum A slender plant with spikes of purple-centred, dark yellow flowers and dark green foliage. 90 cm (3 ft).

olympicum A large and dramatic, distinctly woolly plant. Soft yellow flowers emerge from woolly, white stems above a rosette of large, felted leaves. It is ideal for drier soils. 180 cm (6 ft).

VERBENA *bonariensis*

A marvellous plant for growing between mound-forming perennials. It throws up long, slender, slightly sticky stems that bear just the odd linear, deep green leaf. At the top, widely branched stems carry flat clusters of tiny, pure purple flowers. These are richly coloured and make a fine combination with pink flowers. A short-lived perennial, it should be allowed to seed around, as the seedlings will create a natural rhythm throughout a border. It is ideal for well-drained soils, in sun or partial shade. Summer. 150 cm (5 ft).

Verbascum 'Helen Johnson'

Verbascum chaixii 'Pink Domino'

Verbascum nigrum

Verbena bonariensis

Verbascum olympicum

Veronica 'Ellen Mae'

Veronica austriaca 'Crater Lake Blue'

VERONICA (Speedwell)

Some plants are essential for mixed herbaceous borders, provided the soil is right, and veronicas are one of them. They are not particularly long flowering but are ideal for the front of a border. They produce delicate spikes of little, single flowers and oval, mid-green leaves that can be categorised into two different types. One type forms a weed-excluding mat of foliage, the other a mounding hummock. All need to be grown in a soil that does not dry out during summer, in sun or partial shade.

austriaca **'Crater Lake Blue'** A plant with short spikes of bright blue flowers produced above a spreading mound of mid-green leaves. AGM. Summer. 30 cm (1 ft).

'Ellen Mae' I must be allowed a little vanity here. This was discovered in our herbaceous garden at the nursery in Albrighton. It forms a round mound with small, mid-green leaves and produces short, upright spikes of soft lilac-pink flowers. Although it has a rather short flowering season, it is delightful planted in a small corner with *Fragaria* 'Red Ruby'. Spring. 30 cm (1 ft).

gentianoides This produces slender spikes of sky blue flowers above a dense carpet of shiny, evergreen, deep green leaves. It is a particularly early-flowered variety that resents dry soil. AGM. Late spring into early summer. 45 cm (18 in).

gentianoides **'Variegata'** This is like its sister, *V. gentianoides*, but less robust. It produces deep green leaves, liberally splashed with cream, and sky blue flowers. Late spring. 30 cm (1 ft).

'Pink Damask' An upright plant with long, slim spires of pure pink flowers borne above a mound of mid-green leaves. 90 cm (3 ft).

Veronica 'Pink Damask'

Veronica gentianoides

Veronica gentianoides 'Variegata'

Veronica spicata

Veronica spicata 'Icicle'

spicata This is a most useful border plant. It produces slender spires of tiny, bright blue flowers that appear above a tidy clump of mid-green leaves. Midsummer. 60 cm (2 ft).

spicata 'Icicle' A white-flowered variety with a creeping hummock of fresh green leaves. It really does need a moist soil. Midsummer. 60 cm (2 ft).

VERONICASTRUM

These very handsome, structurally elegant plants are ideal for the back of a mixed border with moist soil. Its leaves are pointed, dark green and carried, like a symmetrical scaffolding, all the way up its tall, very erect, red-tinted stems. These terminate in slender spikes of very small, tubular flowers that emerge from buds of a different colour. Grow in any soil that does not dry out, in sun or partial shade. Midsummer to late summer.

virginicum album Spires of white flowers, with pink buds. 150 cm (5 ft).

virginicum 'Apollo' Soft lavender flowers and white buds. 150 cm (5 ft).

virginicum 'Pink Glow' Soft pink flower spikes, with white buds. 150 cm (5 ft).

Veronicastrum virginicum album

Veronicastrum virginicum 'Apollo'

Veronicastrum virginicum 'Pink Glow'

Viola cornuta

VIOLA

A large and pretty family that ranges in size from the large-flowered pansy to the small, humble violet. They are lovely for scattering around beds and borders of both perennials and shrubs. Although they are generally short-lived, these two varieties will seed around if allowed to do so. Grow in any well-drained soil, in partial shade. Spring to late summer.

cornuta A spreading carpet of light green leaves is smothered for months with daintily shaped, pansy-faced, lilac flowers. A white-flowered form is also available. This is ideal for the front of a border. 15 cm (6 in).

riviniana A clump-forming plant with heart-shaped, richly coloured, green-purple leaves and little, violet-like flowers of deep violet-purple. Let it self-seed. 15 cm (6 in).

WALDSTEINIA *ternata*
(Golden Strawberry)

One of the first perennials to bloom and a much overlooked one. It produces bright yellow flowers, like those of the strawberry, in sprays just above an evergreen carpet of shiny, round, dark green leaves. It is an ideal plant for growing beneath shrubs, but requires a soil that does not dry out, in sun or partial shade. Early spring. 15 cm (6 in).

Viola riviniana

Waldsteinia ternata

KEY WORDS

Bracts These are the leafy bits found at the base of a flower. Good examples can be found around the tiny blooms of *Euphorbia*.

Biennial These are plants that live for only two years.

Bulb/bulbous A bulb can be found at the base of bulbous plants. They store the food needed for growth and are, in fact, swollen, underground buds surrounded by tightly packed layers of fleshy scales.

Calyx/calyces These are found on flowers and are a collection of sepals.

Crown Certain plants grow from the crown, which is at the base and is where the stems emerge.

Cultivar These are plants that originate as a result of cultivation, rather than in the wild. Within a plant name they are identified thus: 'Nora Barlow'.

Genus This refers to the general botanical group the plant belongs to, i.e. *Achillea*.

Hybrid Plants that are hybrids are the result of crossing two species. They generally do not come true from seed.

Leaf node This refers to where the leaf joins the stem.

Mulch A mulch is a top-dressing applied to the soil around a plant. It is a means of retaining moisture during summer, protecting a plant from cold during winter, and also prevents the growth of weeds.

Panicle This term refers to a specific way a plant produces its flowers. These are usually small and carried in short sprays. The flowers are attached to the main stem by short stalks and these together often appear as one unit.

Pinnate This applies to a collection of leaflets that are attached to the main stem in rows, rather like the oars of a boat.

Rhizome These are plants with thick, sturdy roots that tend to lie on or just below the ground. Bearded Irises are rhizomous plants.

Rosette I use this term in two ways. In the case of leaves, it is used to describe how they emerge from the soil. With flowers, it refers to the formation of the petals. In both cases, it is a descriptive way of saying 'in layered circles'.

Sepals These are the leaflike or petal-like parts that can be found just below the petals, and are called collectively the calyx. They exist to protect the petals.

Serrated This refers to the edge a leaf when it is cut into small, jagged teeth.

Species This is the wild form of a plant and can be found in a plant title after the genus. Not all plants have a species name, but if it exists it is written thus: *orientale*, as in *Papaver orientale*.

Spike I tend to use this not in the botanical sense, but in an illustrative way. Technically, these are plants that produce a mass of stalkless flowers, each attached to a central stem. However, I use the term in a literal sense. This is where a lots of flowers, with or without stalks, are produced on one stem form that looks like a pointed spike.

Spurs This is a part of the petal that is elongated backwards into a long tube. Good examples can be found on aquilegias.

Subshrub These are plants that are woody at the base only and die back each year to the shrubby bit. In spring, they produce soft stems that tend to harden off through summer. They are generally cultivated like perennials.

Umbels This refers to a plant that produces its flowers in an umbrella-like formation. These are usually small and borne on reasonably long stalks that splay out, like the wires inside an umbrella, from the top of a stem.

Variegated These are plants whose leaves consist of at least two colours.

Variant A variant is a plant with characteristics that vary from its normal type; e.g. *Convallaria majalis* rosea. In the *RHS Plant Finder*, and botanically, this is written as *Convallaria majalis* var. rosea.

Whorls This refers to the way a set of leaves or flowers is produced. These form layers at even intervals all the way up the stem.

COMMON NAMES

The common name of a plant makes a plant name easy to remember.
The following is a list of common names used within this book and the Latin name under which it can be found.

Angel's Fishing Rod
Dierama

Avens
Geum

Baby's Breath
Gypsophila

Bachelor's Buttons
Ranunculus

Balloon Flower
Platycodon

Barrenwort
Epimedium

Bastard Balm
Melittis

Bear's Breeches
Acanthus

Bee Balm
Monarda

Bellflower
Campanula

Bellflower
Symphyandra

Bellort
Uvularia

Bergamot
Monarda

Bishop's Mitre
Epimedium

Bistort
Persicaria

Bitterwort
Gentiana

Black Cow Parsley
Anthriscus

Black-Eyed Susan
Rudbeckia

Black Snake Root
Cimicifuga

Blanket Flower
Gaillardia

Blazing Star
Liatris

Bleeding Heart
Dicentra

Blue African Lily
Agapanthus

Blue Star
Amsonia

Border Pink
Dianthus

Bouncing Bet
Saponaria

Bowles' Golden Grass
Milium

Bowles' Golden Sedge
Carex

Bowman's Root
Gillenia

Bridal Wreath
Francoa

Bronze Fennel
Foeniculum

Bugbane
Cimicifuga

Bugle
Ajuga

Bugloss
Anchusa

Burnet
Sanguisorba

Burning Bush
Dictamnus

Butterbur
Petasites

Buttercup
Ranunculus

Calamint
Calamintha

Californian Poppy
Romneya

Campion
Lychnis

Canadian Burnet
Sanguisorba

Cardoon
Cynara

Carline Thistle
Carlina

Catchfly
Lychnis

Catmint
Nepeta

Chamomile
Anthemis

Checkerbloom
Sidalcea

Chicory
Cichorium

Chinese Lantern
Physalis

Chinese Rhubarb
Rheum

Chocolate Cosmos
Cosmos

Christmas Rose
Helleborus

Cinquefoil
Potentilla

Clary
Salvia

Columbine
Aquilegia

Comfrey
Symphytum

Coneflower
Echinacea

Coral Flower
Heuchera

Coventry Bells
Campanula

Cowslip
Primula

Cranesbill
Geranium

Cupid's Dart
Catanache

Dame's Violet
Hesperis

Daylily
Hemerocallis

Dead Nettle
Lamium

Dittany
Dictamnus

Drooping Sedge
Carex

Drumstick Primula
Primula

Dusty Miller
Lychnis

Elephant's Ears
Bergenia

Evening Primrose
Oenothera

Everlasting Pea
Lathyrus

False Helleborine
Veratrum

False Indigo
Baptisia

False Lupin
Thermopsis

False Mallow
Sidalcea

False Solomon's Seal
Smilacina

Fescue
Festuca

Feverfew
Tanacetum

Fleabane
Erigeron

Foam Flower
Tiarella

Fox and Cubs
Pilosella

Foxglove
Digitalis

Fringe Cups
Tellima

Funkia
Hosta

Gardener's Garter
Phalaris

Gayfeather
Liatris

Gentian
Gentiana

Giant Cowslip
Primula

Giant Feather Grass
Stipa

Giant Fennel
Ferula

Giant Scabious
Cephalaria

Globe Flower
Trollius

Globe Thistle
Echinops

Goat's Beard
Aruncus

Goat's Rue
Galega

Golden Rod
Solidago

Golden Strawberry
Waldsteinia

Hair Grass
Deschampsia

Hardy Geranium
Geranium

Helen's Flower
Helenium

Hellebore
Helleborus

Heron's Bill
Erodium

Himalayan Blue Poppy
Meconopsis

Hollyhock
Alcea

Hound's Tongue
Cynoglossum

Ice Plant
Sedum

Indian Physic *Gillenia*	**Lupin** *Lupinus*	**Nettle-leaved Bellflower** *Campanula*	**Perennial Sunflower** *Helianthus*	**Rose Campion** *Lychnis*	**Spring Vetchling** *Lathyrus*
Indian Poke *Veratrum*	**Maltese Cross** *Lychnis*	**New Zealand Flax** *Phormium*	**Perennial Wallflower** *Erysimum*	**Roseroot** *Rhodiola*	**Spurge** *Euphorbia*
Jacob's Ladder *Polemonium*	**Marjoram** *Origanum*	**Obedient Plant** *Physostegia*	**Perfoliate Alexanders** *Smyrnium*	**Royal Fern** *Osmunda*	**St. Barbara's Herb** *Barbarea*
Jacob's Rod *Asphodeline*	**Marsh Marigold** *Caltha*	**Orange Hawkweed** *Pilosella*	**Peruvian Lily** *Alstroemeria*	**Russian Sage** *Perovskia*	**Statice** *Limonium*
Japanese Anemone *Anemone*	**Masterwort** *Astrantia*	**Oriental Poppy** *Papaver*	**Pink Cushion Flower** *Scabiosa*	**Sage** *Salvia*	**Stinking Gladwyn Iris** *Iris*
Joe-Pye Weed *Eupatorium*	**Meadow Cranesbill** *Geranium*	**Orris Root** *Iris*	**Plantain** *Plantago*	**Scabious** *Scabiosa*	**Stinking Hellebore** *Helleborus*
Jupiter's Distaff *Salvia*	**Meadow Rue** *Thalictrum*	**Ostrich Fern** *Matteuccia*	**Plantain Lily** *Hosta*	**Scotch Thistle** *Onopordon*	**Stokes' Aster** *Stokesia*
Kaffir Lily *Schizostylis*	**Meadowsweet** *Filipendula*	**Oswego Tea** *Monarda*	**Plume Poppy** *Macleaya*	**Sea Holly** *Eryngium*	**Strawberry** *Fragaria*
King's Spear *Asphodeline*	**Merry Bells** *Uvularia*	**Ox Eye** *Heliopsis*	**Polygonum** *Persicaria*	**Sea Lavender** *Limonium*	**Sundrops** *Oenothera*
Kingcup *Caltha*	**Michaelmas Daisy** *Aster novi-belgii*	**Ozark Sundrops** *Oenothera*	**Prairie Mallow** *Sidalcea*	**Seal Heal** *Prunella*	**Sweet Coltsfoot** *Petasites*
Knapweed *Centaurea*	**Milk Bellflower** *Campanula*	**Painted Fern** *Athyrium*	**Primrose** *Primula*	**Sedge** *Carex*	**Sweet Rocket** *Hesperis*
Lady's Mantle *Alchemilla*	**Milkweed** *Euphorbia*	**Pampas Grass** *Cortaderia*	**Purple Loosestrife** *Lythrum*	**Shasta Daisy** *Leucanthemum*	**Sweet Woodruff** *Galium*
Lamb's Ears *Stachys*	**Miss Willmott's Ghost** *Eryngium*	**Peach-leaved Bellflower** *Campanula*	**Pyrethrum** *Tanacetum*	**Shield Fern** *Polystichum*	**Switch Grass** *Panicum*
Lenten Rose *Helleborus*	**Monkshood** *Aconitum*	**Pearl Everlasting** *Anaphalis*	**Quaking Grass** *Briza*	**Shuttlecock Fern** *Matteuccia*	**Tansy** *Tanacetum*
Leopard's Bane *Doronicum*	**Montbretia** *Crocosmia*	**Peony** *Paeonia*	**Quamash** *Camassia*	**Sneezeweed** *Helenium*	**Tickseed** *Coreopsis*
Lily-of-the-valley *Convallaria*	**Mourning Widow** *Geranium*	**Perennial Flax** *Linum*	**Queen-in-the-Meadow** *Filipendula*	**Snowflake** *Leucojum*	**Toad-Shade** *Trillium*
Lilyturf *Liriope*	**Mrs. Frizell's Lady Fern** *Athyrium*	**Perennial Honesty** *Lunaria*	**Queen Anne's Lace** *Anthriscus*	**Soapwort** *Saponaria*	**Toad Lily** *Tricyrtis*
London Pride *Saxifraga*	**Mullein** *Verbascum*	**Perennial Night Scented Stock** *Matthiola*	**Red Hot Poker** *Kniphofia*	**Solomon's Seal** *Polygonatum*	**Toadflax** *Linaria*
Loosestrife *Lysimachia*	**Musk Mallow** *Malva*	**Perennial Snapdragon** *Antirrhinum*	**Roman Wormwood** *Artemisia*	**Speedwell** *Veronica*	**Torchlily** *Kniphofia*
Lungwort *Pulmonaria*	**Navelwort** *Omphalodes*			**Spiderwort** *Tradescantia*	**Tree Poppy** *Romneya*

Turtle's Head *Chelone*	Variegated Horseradish *Armoracia*	Water Avens *Geum*	White Helleborine *Veratrum*	Wood Bettony *Stachys*	Yellow Archangel *Lamium*
Valerian *Centranthus*	Virginia Cowslip *Mertensia*	Water Figwort *Scrophularia*	Whorlflower *Morina*	Wood Lily *Trillium*	Yellow Asphodel *Asphodeline*
Valerian *Valeriana*	Wake Robin *Trillium*	Welsh Poppy *Meconopsis*	Willow Gentian *Gentiana*	Woolly Sunflower *Eriophyllum*	Yellow Flag *Iris*
Variegated Ground Elder *Aegopodium*	Wand Flower *Dierama*	White Bachelor's Buttons *Ranunculus*	Willow Herb *Epilobium*	Wormwood *Artemisia*	Yellow Gentian *Gentiana*
			Wolf's Bane *Aconitum*	Yarrow *Achillea*	

BIBLIOGRAPHY

BOND, Sandra, *Hostas*. Ward Lock, 1992.

Handbook of Hardy Plants, written by Claire Austin for David Austin Roses, 1985–98.

KING & OUDOLF, *Gardening with Grasses*. Frances Lincoln, 1996.

JELITTO & SCHACHT, *Hardy Herbaceous Perennials Volume 1& 2*. Timber Press, 1985.

LEWIS & LYNCH, *Campanulas*. Batsford, 1998.

PAGE, Martin, *The Gardener's Guide to Growing Peonies*. David & Charles, 1997.

PERRY, Frances, *Border Plants*. Collins, 1966.

PHILLIPS & BURRELL, *Rodale's Illustrated Encyclopedia of Perennials*. Rodale Press, 1993.

PHILLIPS & RIX, *Perennials, Volumes 1 & 2*. Pan, 1991.

PICTON, Paul, *The Gardener's Guide to Growing Asters*. David & Charles, 1999.

ROYAL HORTICULTURAL SOCIETY, *A-Z of Garden Plants*. Dorling Kindersley, 1996.

STEBBINGS, Geoff, *The Gardener's Guide to Growing Irises*. David & Charles, 1997.

THOMAS, Graham Stuart, *Perennial Garden Plants*, Third Edition. J.M. Dent, 1990.

ACKNOWLEDGEMENTS

The following people kindly allowed me to use their gardens to photograph plants:

Lesley and John Jenkins, Wollerton Hall, Nr. Market Drayton, Shropshire.
Charles Cheshire, Burford House Gardens, Tenbury Wells, Shropshire.
The Lord and Lady Vestey, Stowell Park, Northleach, Gloucestershire.
David Howard, Howard & Kooij, Wortham, Diss, Norfolk.
Paul Picton, The Picton Gardens, Colwall, Herefordshire.
John Ravenscroft, Bridgmere Gardens, Woore, Cheshire.
Nigel and Jane Hanson, The Willows, Trysull, West Midlands.

And finally, I would like to thank the following people for their encouragement and help during the compilation of this book:

Martin Page, Ann Dukes, Diana Perry, Kate McWilliam and those brave souls who help me at the nursery, Steve Palmer, Lin Davies, Jenny Yates and Lesley Lees.